D0801876

WHY
I BELIEVE
IN
JESUS CHRIST

Joseph R. Baskin

BROADMAN PRESS
Nashville, Tennessee

To ANN

a true and faithful helpmate
and
a joint heir in the grace of life

© Copyright 1979. Broadman Press
All rights reserved
4269-29

All Scripture quotations in this book are
from the Revised Standard Version of the Bible,
copyrighted 1946, 1952, © 1971, 1973.

Dewey Decimal Classification: 230
Subject heading: THEOLOGY, CHRISTIAN
Library of Congress Catalog Card Number: 79-7736
ISBN Number: 0-8054-6929-X

Printed in the United States of America

Preface

This book is concerned with a widely questioned subject—the uniqueness of Christianity. The principal challenges to Christianity's claims to uniqueness are described in Chapter 1. The other four chapters give the grounds on which the claims of uniqueness are made. The Conclusion seeks to answer the challenges in the light of the evidence presented.

The question this book seeks to answer is of particular interest to today's college student. It is also of importance to many intelligent laymen in the churches who have had occasion to question if there is really any significant difference in Christianity and other religions. The question of uniqueness must also be dealt with by pastors, teachers, and those seriously involved in the missionary enterprise.

Unfortunately, religious bigotry does exist. I fervently hope that this volume will not provide material that would augment a spirit of prideful boasting and arrogance which is so foreign to the spirit of Jesus. We must avoid the temptation of identifying our understanding of truth with the truth itself in its totality. On the other hand, if we are to be honest, we must have the courage to bear witness humbly to the truth as it has laid hold on us.

Preface

My deep appreciation is expressed to Dr. D. Elton Trueblood. Not only have his writings been deeply meaningful and influential for me, but his personal encouragement and suggestions have been invaluable. True thanks is also expressed to my colleague, Dr. Robert Gardner, for his support and real help in matters of style. They, of course, are in no manner responsible for any deficiencies found in the book.

Inexpressible gratitude must go to my wife, Ann, who has not only typed and retyped the manuscript and rendered much-needed aid in matters of style and arrangement, but has also provided constant understanding and encouragement.

JRB

Contents

1

Challenges to Uniqueness

"Different creeds are but different paths to reach the Almighty. Every man should follow his own religion."

—*Sri Ramakrishna*

Christianity has never understood itself to be just one religion among many. There is embedded in the Christian tradition from the earliest days a note of uniqueness. Christians have believed that their faith deals with unique, once-and-for-all events that have significance for the salvation of the entire world. This belief, which has always been offensive, if not scandalous, to some, is being widely challenged today.

Some maintain that there is no longer any need for religion at all, if one understands by that term belief systems which are expressed in nonscientific language and involve worship of the unseen. Others hold that religion is needed by every culture, and each particular culture develops its own which is appropriate to that culture (and which should not be disturbed by the introduction of "foreign" ideas and beliefs). Still others contend that what we need is to take the good points of all religions and combine them into one, worldwide belief system that would unify all mankind. Finally, there are those who hold that religious beliefs are really unimportant anyway. In this chapter we will examine these challenges to the uniqueness of Christianity. The remaining chapters will make plain certain unique features of Christianity.

One of the principal challenges to the Christian claims of uniqueness comes from *secular humanism*. Nurtured by science, fertilized by positivism, and effectively furthered by the marvels of technology, this philosophy exercises a deep and pervasive influence throughout the modern world. Especially in college and university communities has its influence been widespread. Moreover, since this outlook often is found at the level of unstated presuppositions, its influence is frequently unconscious.

Humanism challenges Christianity's claim to be uniquely true by judging it, along with all other religions, to be mere vain imaginings. The basic principles of secular humanism have been conveniently and boldly set out by Corliss Lamont in his *Humanism as a Philosophy*.[1] The primary concepts may be summarized as follows:

1. Humanism believes that there is no Supernatural. Nature is understood as "the totality of being." It is a "constantly changing system of events which exists independently of any mind or consciousness."
2. Man is only a product of this evolutionary Nature. There is no individual survival beyond death.
3. Ideas have no independent existence, but are derived from the human mind interacting with its environment.

4. Man has the power of solving his own problems successfully by the use of his own reason and the scientific method.

5. Human beings possess true freedom and are, within reasonable limits, the masters of their own destinies.

6. All human values are to be grounded in this-earthly experiences and relationships, and these values are to be sought for all mankind irrespective of nation, race, or religion.

7. Art and the awareness of beauty should receive the widest possible development.

8. Men should work for the worldwide establishment of democracy and peace on the foundations of a cooperative economic order.

Though some might like to plead agnosticism on the first and second points, these principles constitute the "working philosophy" of a great number of modern men. Christianity is not unique for them. It is just another example of how men have made a religion for themselves to provide psychological security in an impersonal world. E. R. Goodenough,[2] in an unpublished paper entitled "The Scientific Study of Religion," expresses it like this:

Man universally sees himself confronted with a universe in which he cannot actually predict or control his security, and where he knows sooner or later he will vanish. In no civilization has man been able to endure this. It was just too much, and it still is. . . . In his terror of uncertainty man has everywhere put a curtain between himself and the universe on which he has painted his pictures of Noah, Adam and Eve, of the cosmic turtle, of God, or whatever. And on it, also, he wrote all the rubrics of his rituals. Within this curtain he felt safe, and the security of religious tradition and faith . . . is the security of our painted curtains.

The humanist contends that this inaccurate and pre-scientific view of the universe will be laid aside when man attains the maturity and the ego strength to face the world as it really is and to accept the responsibility for his own destiny.

A second challenge to the claims of uniqueness of the Christain faith comes from the idea of relativism. *Relativism* is a basic assumption of practically all study of man (anthropology), and necessarily so. It maintains that there are no "absolutes." Something can be called "good" or "bad" only because it is considered to have desirable or undesirable effects in a given situation within a certain value system. These value systems are the creations of societies. They are purely functional and bear no relationship to objective reality. *Objective reality* may be a misleading term since what is "out there" can hardly be experienced and can't be described to ourselves or others without language, which is in itself a means of interpretation, subjectively and socially cre-ated. So, reality is understood merely as what one *experiences as reality.*

Religion, *understood from the viewpoint of relativism,* is a system of beliefs and practices which has been created by a particular culture to provide "culturally prescribed solutions of human social and psychological problems" [3] and to conserve the values which that culture holds dear. The various affirmations and beliefs are not to be judged true or untrue (since reality is only what one experiences as reality anyway), but only as effective or ineffective in conserving the desired values.

Since each culture is different, each culture comes up with its own ways of meeting its problems and conserving its values. Moreover, each religion is "best" for that particular culture—Navajo religion for the Navajos, Islam for Arabs, Hinduism for the people of India, and so forth. Such an approach denies that Christianity can give an interpretation or description of reality that is any more accurate or trustworthy than any other religion. Christianity is simply doing, in its own way, what every other religion is doing—providing a way of personal and social adjustment for individuals and the conservation of values for the society. Any significant uniqueness of Christianity goes out the window, according to this view.

This functional understanding of religion, so popular with anthropologists and sociologists, frequently leads to the position that "religion is all right, if you need it." According to R. H. Lowie, religion is good for the man on the street, but adventurous spirits of men of science and aesthetics can do without it. "If a man's being is *wholly* absorbed in intellectual and aesthetic pursuits, his interests may assume for him the place of spiritual guidance; without immersion in such activity, man had better rely upon the traditional faith." [4]

Such relativism combined with a theoretically agnostic, but practically atheistic, humanism is perhaps the dominant world view of American academia today, though there are some signs that it is proving unsatisfactory even there.[5]

Another factor that has caused some to question the uniqueness of Christianity comes from the *increased awareness of other living religions.* Worldwide television, increased study of other religions in secondary schools and colleges, foreign travel, and cultural exchange have contributed to this awareness. In addition, many non-Christian religions have opened missionary work in the United States. Personal contact with persons of another faith tends to lead to the reexamination—perhaps questioning—of one's own. Many of other faiths are intelligent, cultured, personable, considerate, and spiritually sensitive.

From contact with other religions arises a fourth challenge to the claim of uniqueness for Christianity—the challenge of *religious syncretism* or eclecticism. An example of this approach is the Bahá'í faith, a religion originating in nineteenth-century Persia, but which is exercising a growing influence in America.[6]

The main tenets of this faith may be briefly described. God, whose existence is not to be proved by logic but whose signs are everywhere for those who are willing to see, is in his essence unknowable by finite man. God has revealed something of himself through the messengers whom he has sent. These messengers are the founders of the great religions of the world. Since it is God who sends the messengers (and there is only one God), all the great religions are one in essence. The differences in the religions are due to the different needs of the ages in which the messengers appear. The essence remains the same, but individual laws change with changing conditions. Each revelation is what was needed at that time and causes humanity to advance. By the time of Bahá'u'lláh mankind had advanced to the place where they were able to receive the great revelation that shall unify the world and bring forth peace and the "golden age"—a harmonious society inspired by the grace of God.

This faith is attractive to those who desire a religious affiliation without dogmatism or sectarian spirit. The reasons for its appeal are evident. It recognizes the role, force, and power of religion in the life of mankind. It gives an honored place to all the prophets of the world. It is global in outlook, open to critical search for truth, has a high code of personal and social ethics, and maintains a vision of world unity and peace. Is not this an "ideal" religion? Why shouldn't Christians as well as others forget their claims of exclusiveness and join this worthy effort against godlessness and unrighteousness? Indeed, if religion is valid and there were nothing unique about the Christian faith, this would be a logical step.

There is a fifth idea which tends to deny the uniqueness of Christianity. It is *the idea that religious beliefs are not important anyway;* rather, it's the actions which count. This view is expressed by Radhakrishnan. "After all, what counts is not creed but conduct. By their fruits ye shall know them and not by their beliefs. Religion is not correct belief but righteous living. The truly religious never worry about other people's beliefs. . . . The true reformer purifies and enlarges the heritage of mankind and does not belittle, still less deny it." [7]

These challenges to Christianity's uniqueness are having a telling effect in our time. Nowhere is this more readily seen than in the area of missions and evangelism. Most major denominations have seen a decline in the number of converts in recent years. Many have been forced to cut back on the number of missionaries sent out by the denomination.

The decline in mission is serious because it strikes at the very heart of the Christian faith. Mission is not only one of the vital signs of church health, it is essential for its existence. The much quoted statement of Emil Brunner is true: "The church exists by mission as a fire exists by burning." The decline in mission, moreover, is not just a problem of a missionary program. Elton Trueblood observes that ". . . the entire Christian Cause is at stake. Unless there is real validity in the idea of mission, Christians may as well accept with resignation the frequently repeated conclusion that we are finally living in the post-Christian Age." [8] Christian witness, which is essential to the continuance of the church, is also vital to the health of the individual Christian. Without it the Christian life cannot be full, joyous, and complete. We have been exhorted to witness hundreds of times, with little result. Why?

There are many factors contributing to the decline of world missions and to the difficulty that spiritually sensitive Christians have in witnessing. One factor is surely the question of the uniqueness of Christianity. *If* one religion is as good as another, then why bother with witnessing? *If* the claim of Christianity to be the unique revelation of God cannot be held with intellectual integrity in the full light of day, how can we expect thoughtful, educated Christians to give full support to missions or to engage in witnessing on a day-to-day basis? The import of Trueblood's statement is clear, "The most important crisis in the Christian Mission is not financial, but intellectual." [9]

The issue of the uniqueness of Christianity is an important part of a viable theology of mission and deserves the clearest and most penetrating answer we can give.

2

The Uniqueness of Jesus

". . . there are no analogies to the message of Jesus."

—Joachim Jeremias

Many ask, "Have there not been many great religious leaders who have spoken a word of truth from God? How can Christians claim that their revelation is unique?" Perhaps one could state that Jesus was in some respects the greatest of the founders, but is it too much to claim that he is unique?

This chapter will examine the lives, teachings, and self-concepts of some founders of the world's great religions to see if there is any factual basis for Christianity's claim that its founder is unique.

Zoroaster [1] (660—583 B.C.)

Zoroaster [2] (or Spitama Zarathustra as he is called in the *Avesta*) was born in western Iran. His father's name was Pourushaspa and his mother's, Dughdhova. Before

Zoroaster's seventh birthday he was placed under the care of a wise and learned man. He was continuously opposed by evil forces of demons and wizards until he assumed the "sacred thread" (at the age of fifteen), indicating that he had come of age.

Although relatively little information has been preserved about Zoroaster from his fifteenth to thirtieth year, we are told that he exhibited qualities of kindness and tenderheartedness to both man and beast. These years were probably a period of meditation and reflection when Zoroaster spent much of his time in the solitude of the forest and desert places. There he began to formulate the first general truths out of which his religious system was evolved.

The Zoroastrian tradition indicates that at the age of thirty Zoroaster and some of his family were on their way to the celebration of the spring festival, and as he was crossing the river Daiti, the archangel Vohuman (Good Thought) appeared to him. In a trance he was taken to the presence of the Supreme Being, Ahura Mazda, and his angels. There he was instructed in the basic doctrines of the faith.

When he returned to earth he became a priest and began to preach the doctrines of his religion—Mazda was to be worshiped, demons were to be cursed, the archangels should be glorified. For two years he wandered about from place to place, preaching his doctrines, but he had no positive results. In his rejection he sought and found comfort from Ahura Mazda who gave him (during the next eight years) other visions—conferences with various archangels who enjoined on him special moral duties and obligations to care for animals, plants, water, and other aspects of the physical world. He also was given information about Paradise.

This ten-year period seems to be the time of revelation when he received the faith from the Divine Beings. Toward the end of this period he was attacked by the Powers of Evil who tried to destroy him. When he fought back and threatened their destruction, he was entreated by the Lord of Evil Creation to renounce his worship of Mazda. Zoroaster successfully withstood the temptation. During this period Zoroaster had succeeded in making only one convert—his cousin, Maidhyoi-maonha—but this was a foreshadowing of things to come.

During the next two years Zoroaster was guided to the realm of King Vishtaspa. The court of Vishtaspa was dominated by scheming priests and magicians. Zoroaster sought to convert Vishtaspa to the worship of Ahura Mazda. Vishtaspa was interested, but Zoroaster was opposed by the evil priests and magicians and was subsequently imprisoned. He won his release from prison, as well as the conversion and support of Vishtaspa and his wife, by healing the king's favorite horse which had become ill.

With powerful royal patronage and enthusiastic support, the religion of Zoroaster began to spread rapidly. Many converts, including members of Zoroaster's and Vishtaspa's families, came into the faith. It is not known how far or how fast the religion spread, but it is certain that the land of Seistan was one of the earliest areas to receive the faith. Tradition tells of the spread of the faith to foreign lands. While there is no real evidence that Zoroaster himself traveled outside Iran, he was certainly engaged in winning converts.

The primary content of Zoroaster's teaching has been summarized by J. Duchesne-Guillemin.

> A choice must be made between good and evil, and there is a reward or punishment according to each one's choice and according to his thought, words and actions. There will be a new world in which only the virtuous will have a place. Ahura Mazda, the Wise Lord, is alone worthy of worship, as the creator of light and darkness, and as the father of Asha (Justice), Vohu Manah (Good Thought) and Ārmati (Application). No cult should be given to the daēvas (evil spirits); the sacrifice of oxen is forbidden, and that of *haoma* (a sacred drink) is limited. The cult of fire is to be carried out because fire is an instrument of ordeal and, above all, a symbol of divine justice.[3]

Although this teaching has a definite religious content, it must also be seen in relation to the sociological conditions of the Iran of Zoroaster's day. He spoke in a society that was in transition from pastoral to agrarian economy. The good deed for him was the "care and defense of the cattle, to which is added the duty of extending the area of fertilized meadows at the expense of the nomad."[4] Zoroaster also recognized the needs of the physical body and disclosed certain practical knowledge—medical knowledge, the rites for driving out pestilence, sorcery, and witchcraft, and the curing of disease.

Zoroaster has the reputation of being a miracle worker, but not many actual accounts of wondrous works performed by Zoroaster are preserved. One may recall the healing of Vishtaspa's horse. To this may be added a story related by a twelfth-century A.D. author. Zoroaster was passing a blind man in the village of Dinawar.

He told him to take a plant, which he described, and drop the juice into the man's eyes. When this was done the man could see again.

A special concern of Zoroaster was the spread of the cult of the sacred fire. Fire worship existed in Iran before Zoroaster. He supported it and opposed animal sacrifice. Tradition holds that he caused new temples to be built for fire worship in some places.

Another activity which took much of Zoroaster's time was the Holy War. Prince Vishtaspa was opposed by a rival prince named Arjasp because he would neither continue to pay tribute and revenue to him, nor would he give up his newfound faith, the religion of Zoroaster. Vishtaspa was successful in warding off the attack of Arjasp, and Zoroaster's son, Isfendiar, became a crusader for the faith, spreading it to other areas. A second invasion by Arjasp, however, proved to be fatal for Zoroaster. He was slain at the age of seventy-seven (583 B.C.) by a Turanian named Bratrok-resh.

This brief historical survey has given insight into what may be reasonably known of what Zoroaster taught and did. What can be known of Zoroaster himself? What was he like and what did he think of himself?

As a priest, Zoroaster was familiar with the formulae and prayers which he inherited from ancient times. Most of his surviving words are prayers. He had a longing for knowledge of God, but he was no ascetic or mystic who was content to be alone in communion with God. If alive today, he might be called "a vigorous, active, and optimistic man who looks to a future in which all evils will be eliminated. . . ." [5]

He communicated his message and knowledge to others. He was a reformer of religion and rejected certain practices of the past, such as animal sacrifice and worship of demons. He had a concern for animals and especially for cattle and their care. His practical concern for people was evidenced by his disclosure of practical knowledge, e.g., curing of diseases, counteraction of wolves. He was not only a religious reformer, but also a social reformer. He needed a ruler who would follow his practices and put his policies into effect.

Zoroaster saw himself as both a priest who gave right praise to the Wise Lord (Gatha 50:4,9) [6] and as a prophet (50:6) who would speak the truth of the Lord. He felt that he had been chosen by the Lord for the revelation of the truth (46:3, 44:11). Zoroaster heard Good Mind say that he was the only one who had heard their teaching (29:8). He was a "friend" of the Lord (44:1). He asked for a revelation which would put all men to the choice (31:3). The prophet said that whoever heard and followed him would be rewarded now and in the future life (46:10-12,13,18-19). He prayed that he might "be one" with the Wise Lord so his word would have power. He felt that to worship the Wise Lord was his greatest good (51:22); therefore, he brought his own life to the Wise Lord as an offering (33:14).

Buddha (c. 560—c. 480 B.C.)

Siddhattha Gautama [7] (later called the "Buddha," "the Enlightened One") was born in the northern region of India (present-day Nepal) near the town of Kapilavatthu. His family belonged to the tribe of Sakya, a small aristocratic group which existed on the outskirts of the principal Indian monarchies. Siddhattha's father, Suddhodana, was a wealthy landowner. His mother, Maya, died soon after he was born, and Siddhattha was cared for by his mother's sister, another wife of Suddhodana. Siddhattha grew up in Kapilavatthu, the capital of the Sakya realm. We know very little of his childhood. A stepbrother and stepsister are mentioned, but we do not know even their ages in relation to Siddhattha.

It was common for families of Siddhattha's status to have three residences—one for winter, one for summer, and one for the rainy season. Tradition has it that Siddhattha spent his early years in three such palaces. Tradition also holds, and there is no reason to doubt it, that he was married and that he had a son.

In early adulthood (at the age of twenty-nine, according to tradition), Siddhattha left his family and his wealth to seek release from the suffering which usual existence entails—sickness, old age, death. The path which he followed in trying to obtain this release was asceticism, a common practice for young men of his day.

Seven years are said to have passed between Siddhattha's leaving home and his enlightenment, i.e., his attaining of Buddhahood. His first attempt was to submit himself to two successive teachers who guided him through the rigors of asceticism to try to get the spirit "to divest itself of all concrete subject-matter, of every entity, of every conception." [8]

Having failed to find what he was seeking, he left the teachers and went to a wooded spot near the town of Uruvela where he spent some years in the practice of severe discipline on his own. Still he did not receive enlightenment. He increased the severity of the discipline, holding his breath and denying himself nourishment. Five other monks who lived nearby were impressed by his zeal and began to watch him to see if he would attain release by a path which they could follow. They were disappointed when Siddhattha failed to find enlightenment through asceticism and began to take nourishment freely again, so they left him alone.

Enlightenment came, however, some time later as Siddhattha was sitting under a tree meditating. Oldenberg describes it:

> Sitting under the tree, since then named the Tree of Knowledge, he went through successively purer and purer stages of abstraction of consciousness, until the sense of omniscient illumination came over him: in all-piercing intuition he pressed on to apprehend the wanderings of spirits in the mazes of transmigration, and to attain the knowledge of the sources whence flows the suffering of the world, and the path which leads to the extinction of this suffering.[9]

At this moment Siddhattha Gautama became the Buddha, the Enlightened One. He is reported to have said, ". . . and when I beheld this, my soul was released from the evil of desire, released from the evil of earthly existence, released from the evil of error, released from the evil of ignorance. In the released awoke the knowledge of release: extinct is re-birth, finished the sacred course, duty done, no more shall I return to this world; this I knew."[10]

This quote involves some conceptions that may appear strange to the Western mind. To understand them we need to view the background of the dominant religious outlook of that day. Buddha accepted (with some modification) the common Indian belief in *samsara-karma. Samsara,* the doctrine of rebirth, is the belief that the soul is transmitted from one body to another until one finally attains *Nirvana. Karma* is the moral law of cause and effect that determines the particular body into which the soul is born. Buddha modified this belief by denying the existence of a separate entity called "soul," but held to the idea of the necessity of being reborn until the person gains release from the cycle of rebirths. To attain *Nirvana,* then, means that one does not have to continue to be reborn again and again.

The message of Buddha concerned the way that one could gain release from the cycle of rebirths and thereby from suffering of all kind. This message is contained in the "Sermon at Benares." The "Four Noble Truths" delineated in that sermon comprise the basic core of Buddhist doctrine, and it is generally accepted that they reflect the real teaching of Buddha. These truths may be briefly stated as follows:

(1) All of life involves suffering.

(2) The suffering is caused by desire which cannot be permanently satisfied, since nothing is permanent.

(3) There is a method for the elimination of suffering.

(4) The method is to follow the Eightfold Path of right knowledge, right thought, right speech, right conduct, right livelihood, right efforts, right mindfulness, and right concentration. Following this path will lead to *Nirvana.*

After Buddha's enlightenment the tradition provides us with much more information concerning his activity. He at first stayed at the tree in meditation for some days. Here he was tempted to go immediately to *Nirvana,* the state of complete and permanent release. He resisted the temptation, however, and decided that he would first help others to find the way of release which he had found.

His first preaching is presented as taking place in a park at Benares. His audience was comprised of the five ascetics who had formerly deserted him because he abandoned the ascetic severities at the forest of Uruvela. They were converted to his teachings. Other conversions soon followed. The new converts were sent out to preach the message of the path to enlightenment. Thousands were converted—some to full membership in the monastic order, some to the status of lay supporters.

Although the sources do not provide us with adequate material to reconstruct the life of Buddha during the years between his enlightenment and his death, some information is available. It is reasonable to assume that Buddha and his disciples spent the rainy season together in study and discourse and then, when the weather permitted, they would begin itinerating again. Wealthy patrons provided places for the group to stay and teach. One of the most famous of these was a garden named Jetavana given to Buddha by a wealthy merchant. Many people of all stations in life came to hear him.

Though the stories in the Buddhist scriptures consistently present Buddha as one who triumphs over all with his ever-victorious teaching and miraculous deeds, it is probable that he encountered some opposition. His low opinion of the value of Vedic sacrifices did not endear him to the Brahman priests, though there does not seem to have been any organized effort on their part to oppose him. Perhaps greater opposition came from leaders of rival ascetic sects. These attacked Buddha's teaching because he rejected rigorous asceticism as a way to enlightenment. Buddha encountered opposition not only from without, but from inside his own ranks. His own cousin, Devadatta, sought unsuccessfully to wrest the leadership of the community from Buddha's hands.

The year of Buddha's death (c. 480 B.C.) is one of the most certain dates in the history of ancient India. There exists a connected and generally trustworthy account of his death and the events immediately preceding it. Buddha left the Magadha territory where he had been laboring and went northward. He was attacked by a severe illness near the town of Vesali, but he fought it off so he could deliver one last discourse to his disciples. After summarizing his doctrine and admonishing his disciples to be watchful, he set out accompanied by a large group of followers for Kusinara where he would enter into *Nirvana*. There, underneath two sal trees, Buddha made his last bed. After speaking comforting words to his disciple Ananda, he said to all the disciples who were gathered round him, "Hearken, O disciples, I charge ye: everything that cometh into being passeth away: strive without ceasing." Having thus spoken, he passed through various stages of ecstasy and (according to Buddhists) entered into *Nirvana*. The next day the nobles of Kusinara burned Buddha's body with royal honors.

Although the voluminous material concerning Buddha's words and deeds is variously evaluated as to historicity, many scholars think that a trustworthy picture of at least some of Buddha's personal characteristics may be obtained.[11] It is clear that Buddha was a man of great intellect. He was an independent and vigorous thinker. Though he might not have had great originality of ideas, he did have sharp discriminatory powers and would accept nothing merely because it had the authority of tradition behind it. Something must be personally convincing to be accepted as true. He was able to pursue an idea with great persistence and to exclude extraneous matters which might cloud the issue. He followed an idea to its logical conclusion.

His rationality is connected with another characteristic—his equanimity. He is pictured as responding to circumstances in a rationally controlled way so that nothing was allowed to disturb his tranquility and evenhanded dealings with others. This imperturbable equanimity allowed him to be a perfect gentleman at all times. He was a model of urbanity and politeness.

Buddha was not only a thinker and a gentleman—he was also a leader and a man of action. He was busily engaged in teaching and the guiding of his monastic order. He was a man of compassion who actively showed his concern for others. He guided his order with a kind of authority, but it was the authority of a teacher, not of a Lord. He did not "order," but rather "suggested." The type of authority he exercised grew out of his self-concept.

Buddha conceived of himself primarily as a teacher. "The Buddhas [12] are not redeemers, messiahs, saviors, incarnations, or avataras—primarily the Buddhas are teachers who have discovered a great truth which, out of great compassion toward all beings, they teach." [13] Buddha himself said to his disciple, Ananda, shortly before he died, "Ananda, I have fulfilled all the duty of a real teacher. . . . Lead the holy life, you will make an end to suffering. Be a light unto yourself, a refuge unto yourself; let the *Dhamma* [law, teaching] be your only light, your only refuge, and naught else." [14]

The fact that Buddha conceived of himself as only a guide or a teacher who had discovered the "way" may be seen in two other quotes from him. "Whether the Buddhas arise or not, the truth remains unchanged," and "you yourselves must exert; for the *Tathagatas* [the Perfect Ones] but point out the way." [15]

Confucius (c. 551—479 B.C.)

Confucius [16] was born in Tsou, a town in the state of Lu which is near the modern city of Ch'ü-fu in southwestern Shantung Province. The names of his parents are unknown. They were probably members of the minor nobility who had been reduced to a humble status.

It is not clear how Confucius received his education, but he became one of the most learned men of China in his day. He probably received the rudiments of his education as an apprentice doing clerical work. In a society where books were not easily accessible Confucius came to know many historical documents, memorized the *Book of Poetry* (about 300 poems), and became an expert on ritual.

The feudal society in Confucius's time was near a state

of chaos. Corruption, civil war, banditry, torture, assassination, mismanagement, immorality, and incompetence were the order of the day. Confucius wanted to be a man of influence in order to improve society, as well as for personal reasons.

Since he was not personally suited for a career in political intrigue or war, and since he could not bring himself to try to win the favor of a prince by flattery, he decided to seek to gain prominence through vast learning. The problem that Confucius encountered, however, was that the rulers did not at first recognize the value of having a man of great learning and integrity directing the affairs of their territory. Consequently, Confucius began to be a teacher and attempted to transmit his ideas to others.

The number of the disciples of Confucius is unknown. The *Analects* mention twenty-two, and other sources increase the number. Some of these disciples were probably from aristocratic families, but others were not. Once they had been accepted as students they were all treated justly as their attainments deserved. Most of Confucius's disciples were training for political careers, and he helped many of them obtain suitable jobs afterward. Because their schooling included history, poetry, and ritual, as well as principles of government, graduates from the Confucian school proved successful and useful to rulers.

For many years Confucius himself did not have a governmental position. Sometime between 502-492 B.C., however, he was asked to take and accepted a position with a family of the province Lu. The exact nature or title of the position is not known, but Confucius evidently thought that he would have an opportunity to put his doctrines into practice. He was disappointed, however, that he was not consulted as frequently as he thought he should be.

Because he was not used enough, Confucius, although nearing the age of sixty, left the province of Lu and set out on a journey to seek someone who would put his principles into practice. He was treated in different ways during his travels. While most rulers received him courteously and listened politely, they did not offer him a job. Some offers of positions were forthcoming, but never any that Confucius felt he could accept. On one occasion there was an attempt on his life. Finally Confucius came a second time to the province of Wei where he was given a stipend by the Duke who followed Confucius's advice to some small degree.

While Confucius was in Wei some of his friends from Lu sent for him and asked him to return. Although the promised position was not the type he desired, he consented to return. At least he would be among friends and disciples. Here he probably did some editing of written materials, counseled his disciples, and tried, largely unsuccessfully, to influence the affairs of state. Some of Confucius's disciples were dying out. The ones who were left were not very promising. Confucius felt that he had largely been a failure.

Although we do not have a trustworthy account of Confucius's death, we may assume that he faced death with equanimity. During a previous illness when it seemed that the sage was at the point of death, a disciple asked if he wanted him to pray for him. "Is it done?" asked Confucius. When assured that it was customary,

Confucius smiled and said, "My kind of praying was done long ago." [17] After his death in 479 B.C. his remaining disciples spent three years near his grave, mourning the death of their revered teacher. They then scattered to various places of service and perpetuated the teachings of their master.

Confucius's main concern seems to have been helping people to be happy. He saw the primary cause of unhappiness to be improper conduct arising out of improper attitudes and goals. This was especially true in respect to the rulers, since the rulers determined the conditions of the lives of the remainder of society, and since the rulers of Confucius's day were so corrupt. Confucius desired to improve the lot of society by improving the government. He sought to improve the government mainly by improving the people who were responsible for the administration of the government.

What qualities did Confucius desire his disciples to develop? He wanted them to be followers of the "Way," the ideal way of life for the individual and the state. The Way is a kind of natural law that includes "all the virtues, sincerity, respectfulness, justice, kindness, and the like." [18] The Confucian ideal was an educated gentleman who was utterly sincere and who expressed his sincerity by acting virtuously and in good taste. Education (which included music, poetry, and etiquette) was a continuing process, and the Confucian student was to be ever-learning, flexible, open to correction, and always improving himself.

Devotion to the Way was to be expressed in courageous action, even if it caused hardship and suffering for a person. The gentleman was to be modest and avoid undue talkativeness. He was to be loyal to his superior and to be above acting from selfish motives to increase his own wealth and position. He sought to treat others as he would want to be treated.

Confucius did not make much of what is usually thought of as religion. He apparently believed that the universe was sympathetic to right actions, but did not teach that virtue is always rewarded with success. It would, however, always bring a person peace of mind, which was more valuable. He has surprisingly little to say about Ultimate Reality, or about spirits, or about the possibility of life after death. Typical of his attitude towards such matters was his reply when asked by one of his disciples about death. "You do not yet understand life; how can you understand death?" He refrained from raising fundamental religious issues because he did not think they were relevant to the reforms that he was seeking to effect.

Confucius was a powerful personality. Many traits of the man are still visible after more than two thousand years. The impact which he made on his disciples was intense. The fact that he has had such tremendous influence, though he did not appeal either to the will of God or the nature of Ultimate Reality to support his teachings, indicates something of the impact of his own example and the force of his own personality.

Confucius was definitely a teacher rather than a prophet. He did not speak for God, but forcefully taught practical, common-sense ways. He was himself humble, modest, and teachable. He readily admitted his mistakes when shown to be wrong. If a student disagreed with him he was not upset by it, and if he could not convince him by reasoning, he would not try to force agreement by appeal to authority or tradition.

Confucius taught much by example; he was a true embodiment of the ideal gentleman which he held out as a model for his students. He was kind, thoughtful, respectful; he was courteous without being flattering. He was not given to much or extended speaking and was honest and straightforward, at times almost to the point of being blunt. He was generally reserved, but not stiffly formal. His manner was pleasant, and he enjoyed leisure activities, especially music (he played the lute and took part in group singing). A sense of humor is evident in many of the sayings of Confucius. Although Confucius was well-balanced, he was still a human figure who could lose his temper on occasion. He showed much grief when his favorite disciple died. The general picture of Confucius which emerges is of a man of tremendous integrity who is the best example of his own teachings.

Confucius thought of himself as one who had an important work to do in saving society from chaos and corruption. His method of saving society was not through the revelation of some new knowledge or the doing of some great deed, but by learning the virtues of the past and getting them inculcated in and practiced by the people of his own day. This he sought to do through education and political influence.

Jesus (6–4 B.C.—30 A.D.)

Jesus [19] was born in Bethlehem, Judea, during the closing years of the reign of Herod the Great, ruler of Judea

(37—4 B.C.). He grew up in the little town of Nazareth
in Galilee. We have little information concerning him
until he was about thirty years old.

We are told, however, by Luke of an episode in Jesus'
life at the age of twelve when Jesus went to Jerusalem
with his family for the Passover. Here he showed unusual
interest by asking questions of the Temple teachers and
unusual wisdom in answering their questions. He spoke
of the Temple as his "Father's house" in a puzzling
way. We are told by Mark that Jesus had four brothers
and at least two sisters (6:3). Jesus apparently learned
the trade of carpentry from Joseph, Mary's husband,
and when Joseph died it seems probable that Jesus assumed the responsibility for the support of his family.
We may infer that he learned to read in the local synagogue which also, along with his home, transmitted to
him the sacred tradition of the Jewish people.

The canonical Gospels take up the story of Jesus again
when he was baptized by John, a prophetic preacher
who was telling the Jews that a great crisis was coming
and that they should prepare for it by turning to God
and being baptized as a sign of forgiveness. Jesus was
baptized by John. At his baptism he received an influx
of the Spirit of God and heard a voice from heaven,
saying in the words of the Old Testament (Ps. 2:7, Isa.
42:1), "Thou art my beloved Son; with thee I am well
pleased" (Luke 3:22). The influx of the Spirit was an
equipment of Jesus with divine power, and the voice
indicated that Jesus was the beloved Son of God.

After his baptism, Jesus went directly into the isolation
of the wilderness. Apparently he was seeking to understand the meaning of his baptismal experience and to

discern the course that God would have him follow in the future. Satan tempted him. Jesus overcame the temptation (the suggestion that Jesus try to use miraculous powers to satisfy his own needs or to win a popular following). He rejected the path of political power gained through ungodly means and chose to carry out his work by preaching, teaching, and healing.

The theme of Jesus' preaching and teaching was the kingdom of God—the effective rule of a righteous, loving, and personal God. Jesus proclaimed that the time of preparation and waiting was fulfilled, and the time was near when God would bring about his effective rule. Men should turn from their sin and believe the good news of the coming of God's saving activity.

God's saving activity would be fully manifest in the future, but it was evident already in the mighty works of Jesus. Demons were cast out of people. Men suffering from all manner of diseases were made well by his touch or his word. These were signs of the saving activity of God operating in Jesus.

As his many parables make clear, Jesus taught that participation in the kingdom of God was *the* supreme value and that no sacrifice was too great to enable one to enter it. Nevertheless, one could not earn the kingdom; it must be received as a gift, humbly and simply as a child. This reception, however, did demand a decision, a decision to receive the gift, a decision to believe the good news and order one's life accordingly.

The other leading ideas in the teachings of Jesus were closely related to the rule of God and basically made plain its meaning and implications. The God who was bringing the kingdom was preeminently a God of love who loved all men. Now even the outcasts and sinners could find forgiveness and acceptance. This love of God, however, was not mere sentimentality. He demanded complete obedience to his commands, and those who would not repent would perish. The same love and forgiveness offered to men by God was to characterize men's relationships with each other.

The theme of the kingdom of God is intimately related to the phenomenon of discipleship to Jesus. The disciples are the community "subordinate to the kingly rule of God . . . and the ministry of Jesus is the means by which this community is brought into being." [20]

The twelve special disciples whom Jesus appointed were to be the nucleus of this new community, the foundation members of the new people of God. To the disciples Jesus gave special instructions about the "mystery of the kingdom," about the nature and will of God, about prayer, about how the new people of God were to live, and eventually, about the necessity of his coming death.

It is not surprising that Jesus came into conflict with the leaders of his nation. Religiously, his whole approach to living was different from theirs. The most popular leaders (Pharisees) thought that it was by defining the law to cover every life situation, and then obeying it to the letter, that God was to be pleased. Jesus, on the contrary, reduced all the Commandments to two (love of God and neighbor) and taught that the weightier matters of love, justice, and mercy took precedence over the various elaborations of the rules of religion.

Furthermore, Jesus taught that goodness was not measurable by any yardstick. Goodness was qualitative, not quantitative. One came into right relations with God, not by piling up good deeds of which he could be proud, but by humble recognition of his need, acceptance of God's mercy and rule which the coming kingdom offered, and a willingness to treat others in the way that God treated him. Consequently, the whole apparatus of traditional regulations became of no importance.

The Pharisees resented this teaching which they felt to be destructive of the very core of their religion. They also resented how Jesus ignored their regulations in order to help people and to be friends with the outcasts and the socially unacceptable. They were outraged by his claim that God also accepted the outcasts. They resented Jesus' popularity. Jesus criticized their blind legalism and the inconsistencies to which it led, and their failure to give right leadership to the nation.

Jesus was not only religiously undesirable to the leaders, but he had such a popular following he was politically dangerous. The priests of Jerusalem (Sadducees) felt that Jesus must be put out of the way to avert the danger of disturbing the peace and thereby bringing Roman reprisals.

Through betrayal on the part of one of Jesus' disciples (Judas) and intrigue on the part of the Jewish leaders, Jesus was arrested, condemned to death, and crucified. He had foreseen the course of events, and at the last supper which he ate with his disciples he interpreted his coming death. He saw it as a means by which a new covenant relationship would be established between God and men. The new covenant would include the forgiveness of sins and renewed fellowship with God. During the crisis of condemnation and crucifixion, Jesus was deserted by his disciples. After the crucifixion he was buried by a man named Joseph of Arimathea in a rock tomb which was then sealed with a large stone.

The story of Jesus in the primary sources of our information about him does not end with his death. They say he arose from the dead. This belief, observes Dodd, is "not a belief which grew up within the church; it is the belief around which the church grew up, and the 'given' upon which its faith was based. So much the historian may affirm." [21] Evidence for belief in the historicity of the resurrection will be given later (*Infra*, pp. 61ff.). Here it is necessary only to point out that our primary sources of information about Jesus assert that he was raised from the dead.

Several personal traits of Jesus are apparent in our sources. He had a genuine interest in people, and apparently enjoyed mixing with various types of persons. He had great sympathy and compassion for people who were in trouble. Dodd notes several characteristics of Jesus' manner of speaking.[22] He frequently spoke in "short, crisp utterances, pungent, often allusive, even cryptic, laden with irony and paradox." Poetic characteristics often shine through. He had a preference for concrete images rather than abstract propositions.

A particularly striking characteristic of Jesus was his authority. He "called" men to leave all and follow him, and they obeyed. He taught with authority ("I say unto you"). He commanded the unclean spirits, and they obeyed him. He had authority over the sabbath and other traditions which his people had received from their elders and even from Moses. He authoritatively pronounced that a person's sins were forgiven and the person was convinced. He had authority over sickness. The authority of Jesus made such an impression on others that more than one asked concerning the source of his authority. Perhaps this question may be answered from a knowledge of the self-concept of Jesus.

Jesus saw himself as one who had a particular mission to fulfill in the world, a mission that set him apart from other men. "I came to cast fire upon the earth; and I would that it were already kindled! I have a baptism to be baptized with; and how am I constrained until it is accomplished!" (Luke 12:49-50). What was this mission that weighed so heavily on Jesus? It involved the proclamation of the message of God's coming kingdom, but that was not all. His mission also included the defeat of evil powers and his suffering for others, a pouring out of his blood for "many." He conceived of himself as the servant of God described in Isaiah 53 whose death had the power to atone for the sins of many.[23] Such suffering was necessary for the establishment of the new people of God. It was to be the basis of the new covenant which Jesus established.

There are texts that indicate that Jesus understood himself to be Son of God in a unique way. We may note first the voice from heaven which Jesus heard at his baptism ("You are my beloved Son") and which his disciples heard at the transfiguration ("This is my beloved Son"). Second, there is the way in which Jesus addressed God in prayer. He called him *Abba,* the same word a child used when addressing his earthly father. It is to be translated, "Dear Father" or even "Daddy." Jesus was the first one to use this intimate form in addressing God.[24]

Third, Jesus actually spoke of himself as "the Son,"

(apparently of God). In Mark 13:32 he says, "But of that day or that hour no one knows, not even the angels in heaven, nor the Son, but only the Father." Hunter comments, "Here the Son occupies a place of lonely splendour, above both men and angels, subordinate only to God Himself." [25] In Matthew 11:27 Jesus speaks explicitly of a relation to God which he has and which is shared by no one else, "All things have been delivered to me by my Father; and no one knows the Son except the Father, and no one knows the Father except the Son and any one to whom the Son chooses to reveal him." Taylor's conclusion seems inevitable, "Jesus was conscious of being the Son of God in a unique sense." [26]

Mohammed (c. 570—632 A.D.)

Though the exact date of Mohammed's birth [27] is unknown, he was born in Mecca near the west coast of Arabia around 570 A.D. His father, 'Abd-Allah, died before Mohammed's birth, and his grandfather became his guardian. When he was six his mother died and two years later his grandfather. Mohammed then was given into the care of his uncle, Abu-Talib.

Little is known of Mohammed's life until he appears as a prophet in Mecca. Life as an orphan was undoubtedly hard in the commercial city of Mecca. Mohammed gained some commercial experience by traveling to Syria with the caravans of Abu-Talib. He no doubt lacked the necessary funds to go into business for himself.

His financial condition improved when he married the wealthy widow Khadijah (Mohammed may have been twenty-five years of age and Khadijah around forty). To them were born children, probably four girls and two boys. Information concerning Mohammed's activities in the years that immediately followed his marriage is sparse. He continued his commercial interests and acquired a reputation for uprightness. He was able to betroth his daughters to some moderately well-to-do men, but he was still excluded from the inner circle of the wealthy merchants of Mecca.

Mohammed's "call" (according to Muslim tradition) came when he was forty years old. He was in the habit of seeking the solitude of the barren, rocky hills near his home. One of the places which he visited was a cave where he would sometimes spend several nights in prayer and meditation.

In his solitude he had two vivid visions which made a tremendous impression upon him. There appeared to him a "glorious Being" standing high up in the sky, near the horizon. He came closer until he was only two bowshots away and communicated to Mohammed a revelation. In the second vision he saw the same Being standing beside a tree in a garden. Mohammed understood this Being to be Gabriel who commissioned him to be the prophet or apostle of Allah. In difficult days he looked back to this vision for assurance that he had been called by God for a special task. The call involved the reception of revelations or messages from God. Until the end of his life he continued to receive messages. He and his followers memorized them, and later they were written down to form the Koran.

The revelations that came to Mohammed were not merely for his private edification. They were to be proclaimed to others. Mohammed's message must be seen against the background of the common religion of Arabia at this time, which was an undeveloped polytheism. The various local deities were usually identified with some large stone. The most famous of these stones was the black stone at the sanctuary of Mecca, which had been the object of worship long before the day of Mohammed. Pilgrims regularly came to Mecca. Four months out of the year were reserved for pilgrimages and trade, when no warfare was permitted. Often immorality, drinking, gambling, and dancing were part of the pilgrimages.

Though there is some disagreement about which ideas received the most emphasis in Mohammed's communications, the main outlines of his teaching are clear. Mohammed taught that God is good and powerful and that he is going to judge men according to their deeds. The good would receive rewards in Paradise, and the wicked who rejected his teaching would be punished in Hell. Man's response to the goodness of God should be one of gratitude and worship, and openhanded generosity to those in need. Above all there should be submission to the will of Allah.

Mohammed's first follower was his wife, Khadijah, who accepted the validity of his revelation and encouraged him in his tasks. Among the important male converts was Abu-Bakr, who was probably already a friend. He became Mohammed's chief lieutenant and adviser. Others also became followers of the Prophet. Most of these were not from the top strata of society.

The majority of the residents of Mecca did not accept the message of the Prophet. They rejected it both on religious and social grounds. Religiously, many were not convinced by his preaching of resurrection of the dead and judgment. They also rejected the monotheism of his teaching, as well as his claim to be God's messenger. Socially, the acceptance of Mohammed's teaching would mean departing from their ancestors' customs and traditions, which they prized highly. Further, if Mohammed were followed, then the present rulers would lose power. The most serious opposition was led by Abu-Jahl, a young man from another clan. Eventually Mohammed had to leave Mecca.

Before leaving Mecca, Mohammed suffered the death of his wife, Khadijah. She had been an indispensable help to him, and so long as she lived he did not take any other wives. Shortly after her death he married a widow, Sawdah, the first of nine other wives which he was to take.

The way was prepared for him to go to Medina, an oasis town about 250 miles north of Mecca. The inhabitants of Medina were composed of numerous Arab tribes, as well as three tribes of Jews. The religious teachings of the Jews served to prepare the Medinans to some degree to accept Mohammed's message. The numerous Arab tribes had difficulty in getting along with each other and needed someone who could act as an impartial judge. Mohammed seemed to be the answer to their needs.

Having become acquainted with him on their pilgrimages to Mecca, several leaders of the Arab tribes in Medina accepted Mohammed's teaching and invited him to come to Medina as their leader. Mohammed accepted their invitation and immediately began to send his followers from Mecca to Medina. He himself emigrated in September of 622 A.D. His "flight" from Mecca to Medina is called "The Hegira." The year of this emigration and consequent founding of an Islamic community became year one of the Islamic calendar.

At first, Mohammed was not the only leader of Medina. He shared leadership with other tribal chieftains and was distinguished from them mainly by his role as prophet and arbiter of disputes. Despite his friendly efforts the Jewish clans did not accept his message.

An important event in Mohammed's life took place during his first year in Medina—his marriage to 'A'ishah, the daughter of Abu-Bakr. 'A'ishah was only nine years old, and the marriage was mainly for political reasons— to bind Abu-Bakr even more closely to Mohammed.

The followers of Mohammed who had come with him from Mecca did not have any fertile farmland in Medina or any other good means to make a living, so they turned to plundering the caravans from Mecca which passed near Medina. This and other factors finally led to a heated battle with the Meccans (Battle of Badr, 624 A.D.). Although heavily outnumbered, Mohammed and his forces were victorious and interpreted their victory to be the result of divine aid and approval. The sword was to become a principal means of winning adherents to Islam.

The citizens of Mecca tried several times to retaliate but were ultimately unsuccessful. With a force of 10,000 men they laid Medina under siege, but Mohammed had so fortified the city that they decided not to attack. During this siege Mohammed realized what a threat it was to have people within the city who were not on his side, so he decided to get rid of the Jewish tribe that remained in the city. (The other two had been expelled.) He had the men killed and the women and children sold into slavery.

To this period belongs the most controversial of all of Mohammed's marriages. Most of Mohammed's marriages (he had five wives at this time) were largely for economic and political reasons. Such factors were probably not absent from his controversial marriage with Zaynab bint-Jahsh, but other factors were also involved. It seems that Zaynab, Mohammed's cousin, was forced against her will to marry Zayd, Mohammed's adopted son.

One day, so the tradition goes, the Prophet went to visit Zayd. He was not at home, but Zaynab met the Prophet at the door. She was scantily clad. Mohammed did not enter, but courteously withdrew, saying half-audibly, "Praised be Allah who changeth the hearts of men." These words were overheard by Zaynab and she repeated them to her husband. He went to Mohammed and offered to divorce his wife, but the Prophet told him to keep her. He did for a while, but later divorced her. A revelation from Allah convinced the Prophet that it was all right for him to marry Zaynab. It may be read in the Koran, Sura 33:37.

> And remember the time when thou saidst to him unto whom God had shown favor, and to whom thou also hadst shown favor, "Keep thy wife to thyself, and fear God"; and thou didst hide in thy mind what God would bring to light and thou didst fear man; but more right had it been to fear God. And when Zaid had settled concerning her to divorce her, we

married her to thee that it might not be a crime in the faithful to marry the wives of their adopted sons, when they have settled the affair concerning them. And the behest of God is to be performed.[28]

Mohammed's power was slowly increasing. Through a series of threats and negotiations (which sometimes involved Mohammed's placing himself in humiliating positions) the Prophet finally became so powerful that the inhabitants of Mecca were won over to his side. He went to the sacred shrine of the Ka'ba, destroyed the idols, and declared that the day of paganism had passed. Henceforth the cleansed Ka'ba was to be a sacred site for the religion of Islam. Mohammed did not engage in the wholesale slaughter of those in Mecca who had opposed him. Rather he showed a remarkable ability to pardon, especially where important and capable people were involved who might strengthen his cause if they were won over to his side.

In the light of Mohammed's victory over Mecca and his growing power, many Arab tribes began to send representatives to Medina to ask for alliances with him. At first Mohammed was willing to make nonaggression pacts with the more powerful non-Muslim tribes. As his power increased, however, he was able to demand, more and more, the payment of alms and the acknowledgment of himself as God's messenger.

The decline of Persia and the Byzantine Empire further added to the increase of Muslim influence. By the last year of his life, Mohammed's religious, economic, social, and political systems provided the unifying force for the great majority of Arabia. He had created a structure which soon became the basis for a vast empire.

In 632 A.D. Mohammed led his first and last pilgrimage to Mecca. This pilgrimage was now a wholly Muslim affair, all nonbelievers being excluded. At the pilgrimage Mohammed declared that the new era had begun. Usury and blood-vengeance would be abolished. Women were to be controlled by their husbands, but were to be treated with kindness and justice under the fear of Allah. All Muslim men were to be treated as brothers. His followers should fight all others until they confessed: "There is no God but Allah."

A few months after returning from this pilgrimage, Mohammed was taken ill by a fever. He requested permission from his eight other wives to spend the remainder of his time in the apartment of his favorite wife, 'A'ishah. Here on June 8, 632 A.D., he died, his head on 'A'ishah's lap.

Since Mohammed is more recent than the founders of other religions which we have studied, we have more information about his personal traits. Even a description of his physical appearance is available.[29]

Mohammed was always busy and arranged his time wisely. He was given to long periods of silence, but when he spoke it was clear and to the point. He was tactful in his dealings with others. Though he was sometimes severe, his usual manner was one of kindness and gentleness. The Prophet was fond of children and often played with them. Personally Mohammed demonstrated such qualities as courage, resoluteness, magnanimity, and considerable administrative ability. He was able to inspire deep loyalty in his followers.

Mohammed has often been accused by non-Muslims

of being a charlatan, driven by lust and greed, who used religion to improve his socioeconomic status and to gratify his own desires.[30] A fair appraisal of the evidence, though, indicates that Mohammed was not a charlatan, but a sincere man. The "revelations" which he gave, he sincerely believed to be from Allah. However far short his actions (especially his teachings on women and marriage) may fall by other standards, his teachings were an improvement on many conditions that existed prior to his time.

It is clear from the creed of Islam that Mohammed understood himself primarily as a prophet. "There is no God but Allah, and Mohammed is his prophet." There is nothing in the preserved sayings of Mohammed that would indicate he thought of himself in any other manner. He was the spokesman for Allah who brought to the Arabs of his day what he sincerely felt to be the revelation of Allah's will.

Ways in Which Jesus Is Unique

We have now concluded our survey concerning the founders of the great religions of the world. To an extent these founders are very much alike. They were all men of sincerity, compassion, courage, and devotion to their task. They all had to fight against the "establishments" of their day. Most of them had personal experiences (call, revelations, enlightenment, and so on) that form a basis for their subsequent activity (Confucius seems to be the exception here). Several of these founders were skillful teachers, and all expressed some artistic ability in the formulation of their teachings.

Despite the similarities, however, there are some significant truths about Jesus which have no real parallel in the lives of the other founders. *First is his sacrificial death.* He is the only founder who consciously died for others. Zoroaster was killed at the age of seventy-seven by a Turanian fighter. Buddha, Confucius, and Mohammed died more or less of natural causes. Jesus' death was recognized by him as being an integral part of his mission, and he interpreted it as an act that was done "for many" in the establishing of a new covenant between God and man. It is a simple fact of history that no other founder of a religion conceived of himself as dying for the salvation of other men.

From a comparative study of these great founders, it appears further that *Jesus had a unique self-concept.* Confucius and Buddha conceived of themselves as teachers. Mohammed called himself a prophet. Zoroaster saw himself as a priest, as the only prophet chosen for the revelation of the truth, and as a "friend" of the Lord. But Jesus spoke of a sonship relation to God which was shared by no one else.

Jesus also exercised an authority that is not seen in the lives of other founders of religions. Confucius saw himself as the transmitter of a tradition; Buddha as a guide to the truth that delivers from suffering; Zoroaster and Mohammed as spokesmen for the Deity; but Jesus said, "I say unto you." He commanded unclean spirits and they obeyed. He pronounced forgiveness of sins to an individual and later commanded him to take up his bed and walk as proof that he had been forgiven.

Finally, the resurrection tradition about Jesus is absolutely

unique in the annals of the history of the founders of religions.
No other founder of a religion is supposed to have been
raised from the dead. Whatever one may make of its
historicity, it is a fact that no other religion makes such
a claim for its founder.

In this chapter it has been shown that—when the lives
of the founders of the world's great religions are exam-
ined in the light of what can be known of them by the
use of the most authoritative and trustworthy guides
now available—Jesus is found to be unique in many significant aspects.

No other founder conceived of himself as dying for
the salvation of other men. No other founder gave any
indication that he felt that he possessed an unshared
sonship relationship to God. Jesus' authority has no parallel in the lives of other founders. And finally, it is
said of no other founder: "He is not here; for he is
risen, as he said. Come, see the place where he lay."
Whatever position one finally adopts concerning religions and the relationship of Christianity to other religions, these historical facts should not be ignored.

3

The Uniqueness of the Bible

"This 'acting' and this 'speaking' took place in Israel and no-where else."

—*Emil Brunner*

The center of the uniqueness of Christianity resides in its Founder, but that is not the whole story. The Bible, the sacred book of Christianity, is also unique. There are three lines of evidence that lead to this conclusion. First, the Bible stands in a unique historical relationship to Jesus. Second, the Bible is linked in a unique way with historical events. Third, the Bible has manifested a unique power to change the lives of persons. Let us examine these lines of evidence.

First, the Bible stands in a unique historical relationship to Jesus. Chronologically the New Testament writings have a position that the writings of no other time can share. They were written in the time which immediately followed the unrepeatable historical events of the life of Jesus of Nazareth. There is absolutely no way any author of the twentieth century, or the fifteenth, or the fourth can duplicate the situation of the authors of the New Testament.

New Testament writings also have a unique geographical and personal relationship to Jesus. They rest upon the testimony of the people who knew him best—the apostles.[1] The testimony of these men who knew Jesus in the flesh, who received his teachings and instructions, and who saw him after his resurrection is of unique value.

Oscar Cullmann draws attention to the uniqueness of the apostolic testimony. The history of salvation, says Cullmann, "has a centre which serves as a vantage-point or norm for the whole extent of this history, and this centre is constituted by what we call the period of direct revelation, or the period of the incarnation. It comprises the years from the birth of Christ to the death of the last apostle, that is, of the last eyewitness who saw the risen Jesus and who received, either from the incarnate Jesus or the risen Christ, the direct and unique command to testify to what he had seen and heard." Thus it follows "that the apostles are not writers like other authors of antiquity, but men set apart by God for the execution of his plan of salvation by their witness, first oral, then written." [2]

The uniqueness of the New Testament, then, arises out of two facts of history: (1) the uniqueness of Jesus of Nazareth and (2) the unique position of the apostles as intimate eyewitnesses of his ministry and his resurrection appearances.

But what about the Old Testament? Its unique relation to Jesus lies first of all in the fact that the Old Testament provides the historical and theological background against which the life and teachings of Jesus are to be correctly understood. Jesus himself was a Jew. The material preserved in the Old Testament largely shaped his thinking. He read the Prophets, knew the Psalms, and was familiar with the Law. The central ideas in the teachings of Jesus are firmly rooted in the Old Testament— the Father God, the kingdom of God, love of God and one's neighbor, obedience to God, trust in God, absolute sincerity and humility, the triumph of suffering love. F. C. Grant describes Jesus' relationship to the Old Testament as one where "the fundamental revelation of God in the Old Testament, and his character and purposes as therein revealed, are everywhere taken for granted." [3]

The relation of Jesus to the Old Testament, however, is not just one in which there is a sharing of common ideas. Both from Jesus' own teachings and the teachings of the apostles, it is clear that there is a dynamic historical relationship between the Old Testament and Jesus. He is the fulfillment [4] of the Old Testament.

First, Jesus fulfills certain Old Testament prophetic predictions. The New Testament writers saw even the details of Jesus' birth, life, death, and resurrection predicted in the Old Testament. If it should seem to those schooled in the historical method of understanding Scripture, that in some cases the Old Testament writers did not have the Messiah in mind when they spoke their words (e.g., Matt. 2:15; Hos. 11:1), there are still many instances where actual predictions are fulfilled in the life of Jesus. Important examples are his birth in Bethlehem (Mic. 5:2—Matt. 2:6), of the line of David (Isa.

11—Matt. 22:41-42; Matt. 1:6), his preaching good news
and bringing healing to the blind, the dumb, and the
lame (Isa. 35:5-6; Isa. 61:1-2—Luke 4:18-21; 7:20-23),
his entry into Jerusalem on a colt (Zech. 9:9—Matt. 21:4-
5), his suffering (Isa. 53—Matt. 26:54-56), and the establishing of a new covenant (Jer. 31:31-34—Mark 14:24).
Though there have been prophets in other cultures,
there is no other case which is comparable to the prediction and fulfillment that can be seen in the Old Testament and the person of Jesus of Nazareth. This statement is not intended to support the vagaries to which
prediction-fulfillment has sometimes been put, but such
abuses should not blind us to facts of history.

Jesus not only fulfilled prophecies about the Messiah
that had been made in the Old Testament, he also fulfilled the *promises* that God had made to the Jewish fathers. Paul says in Acts 13:32-33, "We bring you the
good news that what God promised to the fathers, this
he had fulfilled to us their children by raising Jesus."

Gerhard von Rad [5] has shown how the various promises made to Israel in the Old Testament received only
a partial fulfillment within the Old Testament itself.
Thus the promise of the land of Israel was fulfilled (Josh.
21:43-45), but not completely, for Israel still had to share
her land with the Canaanites (Judg. 2:3,21,23). The dynamic leaders of Israel (Gideon, Samson, Saul) were
called to deliver Israel from her enemies. They succeeded, but only in part, for their failure is plainly re-
corded in the pages of the Old Testament. The promise
of universal rule made to the kings of Judah (Ps. 2, 72,
110) certainly are not fulfilled in Old Testament history.

To these instances of partially unfulfilled promises
may be added the unfulfilled visions of various prophets

of an "age of salvation." The age of salvation would be based on a new covenant between God and his people (Jer. 31:31-34). Also it would be a time when God's Spirit was poured out on all flesh (Joel 2:28-32). A great judgment (Zeph. 1:1; Joel 3) would be followed by an era of universal peace (Isa. 2, 11) when the sick would be healed (Isa. 35:5f, 61:1f) and when all the world would worship the true God (Isa. 2; Ps. 67:2-4). This vision of the future also came to include resurrection of the dead (Isa. 26:19; Dan. 12:2-3) and an eternal kingdom that would not pass away (Dan. 7:14).

Obviously Jesus did not fulfill all these prophecies. Where, for instance, is the universal age of peace where all men worship the true God? It has not yet appeared. What the New Testament writers affirm, however, is not that the age of salvation has been consummated, but that it *has begun.* They see in Jesus clear evidence that *some* of the promises and hopes of the age of salvation *have* indeed happened in history (the healing of the sick, the new covenant, the gift of the Spirit, the beginning of the resurrection), and therefore they expect the remainder to be accomplished by him.

It is now clear that the whole Bible stands in a unique historical relationship to Jesus. The New Testament rests on the testimony of those who knew Jesus best—the apostles. The Old Testament provides the background for his thought and contains both predictions and promises that are remarkably fulfilled in the person of Jesus of Nazareth.

We now turn to the second line of evidence that causes us to judge the Bible to be unique—its unique relation to actual historical events that have really transpired in time and space. The importance of this relationship to history can be seen when one remembers Goodenough's figure of the "painted curtains." [6] His contention is that religion is totally subjective. If man's needs and questions are the only basis of religion, and if there is really nothing in the world *as it really, objectively is* that corresponds to those pictures which he (man) has painted, then religion is merely an illusion. The religious man is a dreamer who is out of touch with reality.

But if a particular set of pictures on the curtain is based on real, historical events—things that have actually taken place—then this is another matter. This is exactly the claim that is made for the biblical set. The great assertions of the biblical faith are not presented as just thought up by man, but as made known by God in and through *his mighty acts.* In fact, it is a narration of the acts and their meaning that forms the principal "pictures" of biblical religion.

As G. E. Wright points out: ". . . to conceive of it [biblical theology] primarily as a series of ideas which we must arrange either systematically or according to their historical development is to miss the point of it all. It is fundamentally an interpretation of history, a confessional recital of historical events as the Acts of God." [7] This is true in both Old and New Testaments.

The Old Testament was written by various members of the Hebrew people. The history of this people may be said to begin with Abraham of Ur, but none of the Old Testament was written until after what many would consider the most decisive and constitutive event in the entire history of Israel—the Exodus from Egypt. In this event (the deliverance of the Hebrews from the bondage

of the Egyptians) the God of the Old Testament was
definitively made known. To those who were delivered
it was proof of God's power and love.

> Say therefore to the people of Israel,"I am the LORD,
> and I will bring you out from under the burden of
> the Egyptians, and I will deliver you from their bond-
> age, and I will redeem you with an outstretched arm
> and with great acts of judgment, and I will take you
> for my people, and I will be your God; and *you shall
> know that I am the Lord your God* [author's italics], who
> has brought you out from under the burdens of the
> Egyptians"(Ex. 6:6-8).

God's activity was so clearly manifest that even the
Egyptians would know that the God of Israel was the
LORD (Ex. 14:18).[8]

To succeeding generations, the mighty act of deliverance that God had accomplished in the Exodus continued to be an event in which God's activity could be
clearly seen. Prophets like Amos (2:10), Micah (6:4-5)
and Ezekiel (20:5-12) pointed to the Exodus as evidence
of a clear manifestation of God which left the Hebrews
with no excuse for failing to worship and obey him.
In addition to the prophets, some of the Psalmists emphasized the revelation of God in his mighty acts (Ps.
78, 136).

Not only in the Exodus and the conquest of the land
of Canaan, but also through Israel's subsequent history,
God made himself known to his people. In their military
victories and defeats the Israelites understood God to
be making himself known (1 Kings 20:13). In the defeat
of Israel by other nations, the prophets saw God express-

ing his judgment on a sinful people. Isaiah believed that the God of Israel alone was in charge of history, and he challenged any other god to offer a satisfactory explanation of history. Because his God is the real God, only his spokesmen can "show the things to come hereafter" (Isa. 41:21-24).

The events of history proved the words of the prophets not to be idle imaginings, but true information concerning the activity of the One who is in charge of history. A recent study of revelation in the Old Testament by the German scholar Rolf Rendtorf leads to the conclusion that, "Throughout it is clear that Jahweh [the LORD] is known in his historical acts to ancient Israel and that in them he manifests himself as he is." [9]

The events that form the core of the biblical story from the patriarchs to the return from the Exile are not imaginary stories, but actual historical events whose reality is generally corroborated by the work of the scientific historian and archaeologist.[10] Just because these events took place does not, of course, make them revelatory. Revelation is God making himself—his will, purpose and nature—known. Factual events become a revelation of God only when someone gives God's interpretation of the event. This is the task of the prophet—one who speaks for God. The relationship between history and revelation in the Old Testament then may be stated thus: the Old Testament revelation comes as the prophet is given to see the divine meaning of the historical events which occur.

Both event and interpretation are essential for historically mediated revelation. Event without divine interpretation would bear no *divine* meaning. On the other hand, a purported divine message or meaning which is not confirmed by the reality of actual happenings is open to the charge of being mere speculation or wish-thinking.

Without the interpretive Word from God the patriarchs would merely be Amorites in search of land, the Exodus just a group of slaves who managed to escape from Egypt, and the fall of Israel an unfortunate result of Babylonian expansion. Without the occurrence of the events themselves, the story which the Bible tells would be imaginary. Emil Brunner summarizes clearly the nature of historically mediated revelation. "This revelation takes place through the 'words' of God and through the 'acts' of God. Both together, equally, constitute the fact of historical revelation." [11]

Historical revelation, we might say then, is revelation that is confirmed by the events of history. The purported divine message is borne out by actual happenings. This is exactly the test the Old Testament gives to distinguish the true from the false prophet. "When a prophet speaks in the name of the LORD, if the word does not come to pass or come true, that is a word which the LORD has not spoken" (Deut. 18:22).

The relationship of event and interpretation which we see operating in the Old Testament story of Israel is not found in the religious literatures of other world religions. G. Ernest Wright points out that "the type of religious literature produced in all those countries—India, China, Persia—is very different from the Bible. The Veda of Hinduism, the Pali literature of Buddhism, the Confucian Classics, and the Avesta of Zoroastrianism are all composed for the most part of liturgical material

and especially of *teachings* on a great variety of subjects.
None of them has any particular historical interest. Even
the Koran of Islam . . . is chiefly a series of teachings
from the auditions and the visions of the prophet
Mohammed." [12]

The relationship of revelation to history which is seen
in the Old Testament is intensified in the New Testament. There are three reasons for the intensification:
(1) the events which are singled out as revelatory are
concentrated in the life of one historical person—Jesus
of Nazareth; (2) the events are such that they are ade-
quately understood only as acts of God; and (3) the
gap between event and the divine interpretation is much
less because the one who gives the meaning of the deed
is viewed as more than a prophet.

The first of these reasons is obvious and needs no
further comment. The other two, however, need to be
explained.

Some of the events connected with Jesus can be ade-
quately understood only as acts of God—his announce-
ment of forgiveness of sins, his miracles, and, above
all, his resurrection. Jesus' opponents rightly recognized
that forgiveness of sins is the prerogative of God alone.
Jesus pronounced a man's sin to be forgiven (Mark 2:5)
and to show that it was not an idle promise he healed
the man's body. If today one asserts that the miracles
of Jesus are indeed historical events, the burden of proof
lies with him. H. Van Der Loos has accepted that burden.
At the conclusion of his monumental study on miracles
(over seven hundred pages in which he investigates the
scientific as well as the historical problems), he states,
"Our study has revealed that we consider the accounts

of miracles in the Gospels to be historically reliable." [13]

That Jesus performed miraculous deeds is well supported historically. One may "explain" the miracles of Jesus in various ways. His opponents suggested that the superhuman power at work in him was of the devil. But do either the works themselves (making men whole), or Jesus' character make that explanation the most likely one?

Some miracles *might* be explained in terms of the concepts of mental illness (demon possession) and psychosomatic medicine (paralysis), but not all of his miracles can be explained in this way (for example, the raising of Jairus' daughter). One is forced to say either that they are "strange, unexplained happenings" or that here "God is at work in an unusual way."

The one event above all others in the New Testament that demands recourse to the supernatural power of God for an explanation is the resurrection of Jesus from the dead. Only God can raise the dead. If Jesus were really raised from the dead, it must have been a direct act of God. If it happened, it is so clearly an act of God that it "proves" his reality and his approval of what Jesus had said and done.

We are maintaining that the Bible has a unique relation to events in history, and that the most important event, so far as the New Testament faith is concerned, is the resurrection of Jesus from the dead. But did it really happen? Since the resurrection as historical event is so important to the uniqueness of Jesus, we must show clearly the historical grounds for believing that it occurred.

The New Testament presents two pieces of evidence

which indicate that Jesus was actually raised from the dead—the empty tomb and the resurrection appearances.

All four Gospels report that the tomb in which Jesus was buried was later found to be empty. The empty tomb is also clearly implied in the earliest account (traceable to six to eight years after Jesus' death) of Jesus' resurrection appearance that we have—1 Corinthians 15. Even the Jews who opposed the apostles recognized that the tomb was empty (Matt. 28:11-13). One scholar forcefully asserts that the claim that Jesus was alive "could not have been maintained in Jerusalem for a single day, for a single hour, if the emptiness of the tomb had not been established as a fact for all concerned." [14] Furthermore, if the disciples had been manufacturing the story about the empty tomb (to support the claim that Jesus was risen) they would scarcely have placed it on the lips of women witnesses because the testimony of women was not very valid, according to Jewish ideas of the time.

In the light of this evidence we are justified to speak of the *fact* of the empty tomb. To assert that the tomb was empty is not the same thing, of course, as to assert that Jesus was raised from the dead. It is, however, corroborating evidence that even the secular historian could verify, and which no historian has been able to refute.

The other piece of evidence which we have mentioned—the resurrection appearances—is more cogent for accepting the resurrection itself as a fact. We may begin with a fact that is accepted by practically all historians: The apostles who had known Jesus before his death claimed that they had seen Jesus alive after he had been

killed and buried. There is unquestioned *written* evidence
of this fact that can be traced to within a few years of
Jesus' death (1 Cor. 15:4; Gal. 1:18). Furthermore, it
is impossible to believe that the apostles made up a
story that they knew was not true, because a person
would scarcely be willing to die for what he knew was
a falsehood.

The apostles sincerely believed that Jesus was raised
from the dead. Were they mistaken? There is no real
doubt that Jesus was actually dead. There is little likeli-
hood that the appearances were hallucinations for the
following reasons: (1) The disciples were not expecting
Jesus to be raised from the dead (Luke 24:11, 21). (2)
The appearances occurred to more than one person.
Paul mentions more than five hundred persons at one
time who had seen the resurrected Jesus, most of whom
were alive when Paul wrote (1 Cor. 15:6). (3) They occurred at more than one time and one place (1 Cor. 15:3-
8). (4) The appearances produced salutary and lasting
effects in the lives of the apostles. (5) Thousands of
people over a period of twenty centuries bear witness
to a type of experience that confirms the reality of that
to which the apostles bore witness.

In summary, the historian as historian can affirm: (1)
Jesus was really dead. (2) The tomb was found to be
empty. (3) The disciples sincerely believed that Jesus
was raised. (4) This was a belief around which the church
grew up, rather than a belief that grew up in the church
(*supra*, p. 38). (5) It is not likely that the appearances
of the resurrected Jesus to his disciples were hallucinations.

If the historian refuses to say that the resurrection

actually occurred, it is more due to his own presupposition, that such a thing could not happen, than to a lack of evidence. The historian's task is to tell what happened and, in so far as he can, explain it in terms of the regular, naturally understood workings of the world. If he is confronted with a happening which he cannot explain by the use of his categories (regular, naturally understood workings of the world), he should *affirm the happening* and confess the inadequacy *of his categories* to explain it. Thus I maintain that the resurrection of Jesus from the dead should be called a fact of history. The statement that *God raised him from the dead* would be an interpretation of the fact, but within the context, the most appropriate interpretation available.

If Jesus was raised from the dead by a direct act of God, this puts him in a class all by himself. If God acted so uniquely in relation to Jesus, then Jesus must have a unique relationship to God. This is exactly the conclusion to which the New Testament writers were led. They came to believe that Jesus was the unique Son of God (Rom. 1:4; 1 Peter 1:3; Heb. 1; John 20:31, 1:18).

If the earthly Jesus of Nazareth is the unique Son of God, the historically mediated revelation reaches its apex in Jesus. In the Old Testament, revelation had come through event and interpretation. Though the revelation was always adequate for God's specific purpose, it was also necessarily limited by the medium through which it came. The interpretation of the acts was limited by the prophet's capacity to receive it. No prophet was capable of receiving the complete revelation of God. The author of Hebrews recognized the partial and fragmentary nature of the revelation which came through the Old Testament prophets and contrasted it to the revelation through a Son, whom he declares to be the exact image of the Father (Heb. 1:1-3).

The New Testament maintains that in Jesus one sees the completely obedient and faithful Son (Mark 14:36; John 8:29; Phil. 2:8) who has unique knowledge of the Father (Matt. 11:27). If Jesus is completely obedient to the Father, then his *actions* express the Father's will. Bernard Ramm has clearly seen this and spelled out its significance:

> The attitudes, actions, and dispositions of Christ so mirrored the divine nature that to have *seen* such in Christ is to have seen the reflection of the divine nature. Christ's attitudes mirror the Father's attitudes; Christ's affections mirror the Father's affections; Christ's love mirrors the Father's love. Christ's impatience with unbelief is the divine impatience with unbelief. Christ's wrath upon hypocrisy is the divine wrath upon hypocrisy. Christ's tears over Jerusalem is the divine compassion over Jerusalem. Christ's judgment upon Jerusalem or upon the Pharisees is the divine judgment upon such hardness of heart and spiritual wickedness.[15]

Of course, we know the intended meaning of Jesus' actions only as they are interpreted by his words. These are not the words of a prophet speaking for God, but of the Son speaking for his Father.

Jesus' words and actions form a mutually enlightening and enriching unity. His words tell what his actions mean, and his actions show what his words mean, and demonstrate that they are not mere words. Jesus interprets his deeds of healing as evidence of the manifestation of the kingdom of God in history. He interprets his coming death as the "blood of the covenant which is poured out for many" (Mark 14:24). In this unity of deed and word which we see in Jesus we have what might be called the "self-interpreting acts of God." The perfectly obedient one makes known from the unique position of his son-relationship the true meaning and significance of his actions.

We may conclude, then, from the evidence which has been presented, that the Bible is intimately related to, bound up with, and confirmed by real history in a way that is true of no other religious book.

The *message* of the Bible is also unique, but since this will be shown in the next chapter, we turn now to another mark of the uniqueness of the Bible—*its power. The power of the Bible can be most clearly seen in its effect on human lives.* The annals of Bible societies, Scripture distribution organizations, and foreign mission boards contain multitudes of examples as to how the Bible has changed the lives of people. A few of these may be related.

Carl E. Bates, one-time president of the Southern Baptist Convention, relates the story of his conversion. He was reared in a Christian environment, but when he finished high school he moved to New Orleans to get a job. There he became involved in gambling and other activities of ill repute. He enjoyed such activity for a while but began to be troubled by pangs of conscience which he attempted to quiet with alcohol.

When it became apparent that he was being unsuccessful in his efforts to gain satisfaction, he seriously contemplated suicide. He would stand for hours beside his hotel window, wondering if he could dive headlong onto the sidewalk below and end his troubles. One evening while he was trying to summon enough courage to jump, his hand fell on a book he had not noticed before. He picked it up and began to read and found that he could not put it down. He came to feel that his trouble arose from his cutting himself off from God.

As this conviction deepened, he knelt by his bed and said, "If You are there and can do something for a guy like me, I want to know it! And if you do anything to make yourself known to me, I promise I will spend the rest of my life trying to convince men that You are real and that You make yourself known. . . . Before I had finished speaking I knew within myself that God was not only a very present reality but that He had lifted the weight of sin that had almost crushed the life out of me." [16]

One might attempt to explain the above incident in terms of a "Christian conscience," rather than of the power of the Bible. Such an explanation could scarcely be offered, though, in the case of Duane Seaborne. He had been brought up on "the wrong side of the tracks" in a non-Christian home. When he enlisted in the navy at the age of seventeen, he did not believe in God and thought that the church people whom he knew were hypocrites.

Assigned to the aircraft carrier *U.S.S. Wasp,* he became disturbed upon witnessing the drowning of several men when their ship had been rammed by the *Wasp.* He wondered what happened to those men who had died. Later that night he picked up a Gideon Bible and started looking for an answer, not really expecting to find one. For two years, off and on, he read until he had completed the book. He says, "By the time I had come to Isaiah 53, I began to sense the presence of God. I don't know how to describe this sensation. All my life I had felt alone and unwanted. I had literally come from the wrong side of the tracks. No one cared if I lived or died. Now as I read the beautiful words of Isaiah 53 . . . I suddenly knew that Someone loved me. I knew that God stood by my side. With this realization, the tears began to pour down my cheeks. . . . The terrible loneliness had gone and in its place was the feeling of peace and joy." [17]

The power of the Bible to bring conviction and to change lives is not restricted to the "Christian" cultures of the West. In Indonesia, a group of local thieves from the village of Payak stole several items from a home. Their loot included several books which were tossed aside because none of the thieves could read.

Some time later, a person who said he could read joined their group. To test him, the other thieves dug out the books. He read from a volume containing stories about a lost sheep, a woman who lost a coin, and a young man who sold his share of his father's property and left home. Their curiosity was so aroused that they decided to go ask the victim of their raid for an explanation of these stories. This ultimately led to their conversion and the founding of a thriving Christian church.[18]

The Bible has power, not only to bring vast changes in the lives of individuals, but there are also examples of Christian communities which have been created in non-Christian cultures—primarily by a Bible. Korea was officially sealed off from the West until 1882, but two

Gospels had been translated into Korean some years before. When at last Western missionaries were admitted into Korea, they found several Christians in Seoul awaiting baptism. They had been converted by copies of a Gospel which had been smuggled across the Manchurian border. A similar situation obtained in the Batak church in Sumatra.[19]

Another example is related by Dr. Baker James Cauthen, former executive secretary of the Foreign Mission Board of the Southern Baptist Convention. According to Dr. Cauthen, a number of years ago Dr. Julius Hickerson was flying back to his home in Barranquilla, Colombia, for a conference relative to the founding of a seminary in that country. The plane crashed in the mountains, and Dr. Hickerson and all the other passengers lost their lives.

After some years, Christian workers going through that part of the country encountered a group of people who were believers. In answer to inquiries about how they heard the gospel, they indicated that no one had come there to preach to them. They brought out a book, a Bible, and explained that they had found it in the wreckage of a plane crash, had read it, and from it had learned what they had come to believe and practice. The name of *Julius Hickerson* was in the Bible.

Clarence W. Hall, a news correspondent assigned to United States troops during World War II, writes of his experience in the small, remote Okinawan village of Shimabuku. When the United States troops came upon Shimabuku they were amazed at the contrast between it and other Okinawan villages they had visited. The streets and homes were spotlessly clean, the villagers were courteous, and a high level of health, happiness, and prosperity prevailed. It was discovered that a Japanese Bible left by an American missionary on his way to Japan thirty years before had become the guiding book for their village society.[20]

The power of the Bible may also be seen in its ability to give strength and help to people in times of crisis and hardship. One incident must stand for the thousands of examples that could be given. Air Force Captain James Ray found himself in a solitary cell in a North Vietnamese prison. Though it was against the rules, he and other prisoners made contact with each other by a chain of whispered messages.

Through this medium they began to teach each other what Bible verses they remembered. They devised other means of sharing the Scriptures with each other—writing verses on toilet paper with brick-dust ink and leaving them behind a loose brick at the toilet, and tapping them out in Morse code on their wooden cell walls. Ray says that the Scriptures became "vital to our daily existence. Often racked with dysentery, weakened by the diet of rice and thin cabbage and pumpkin soup, our physical lives had shrunk within the prison walls. We spent twenty hours a day locked in our cells. And those Bible verses became rays of light, constant assurances of His love and care." The Scripture which they were able to remember was their "secret of survival." [21]

The Bible not only has brought about changes in relatively uneducated people, but some highly educated persons have found in the Bible a message which has become an interpretive center for their lives.

Dr. Otto A. Piper, professor emeritus at Princeton

Theological Seminary, in a series of articles written at the request of the editor of *The Christian Century*,[22] indicated the important influence of the Bible in his life. Born in a religious, middle-class German family in the latter part of the nineteenth century, he received a measure of religious instruction, including the reading of the Bible, but failed to see its relevance.

He became very interested in the Bible, however, when he read a novel about Jesus and became aware that the Bible really had a message for the present day. He decided to become a teacher of religion. At the universities of Jena and Marburg he became acquainted with the historical-critical study but lost interest in what his professors presented as the religion of the Bible. He questioned whether or not to pursue a theological degree.

A year in Paris offered a change of environment in which to try to work through his problems. Of the many influences that played upon him there (philosophical controversies, the sculpture of Michelangelo and Rodin on display at the Louvre, close contact with Roman Catholicism) the most decisive was the theological and devotional life at the Protestant seminary. Here he found an emphasis on social reform growing out of Christianity and discovered "Biblical realism"—the concept that the Bible "teaches not dogmatics but history; namely God's dealings with mankind." He also was impressed with what he saw happening in the lives of religiously illiterate Roman Catholics or free thinkers when the gospel was brought to them by the Huguenot students at the seminary.

After a tour of duty in World War I and completion

of his graduate work, he was appointed to the theological faculty at Göttingen. Here he began to see that the realities which the biblical man dealt with are the same realities that modern man has to deal with, though we might call them by different names. His concern with social, international, and political problems, and his clash with Nazism required a more adequate understanding of the church in the world. This he found in the idea of "holy history" which became central in his understanding of the Bible.

A short stay in England after his expulsion from Germany brought him into contact with the Bible-loving people of Keswick. They opened his mind and heart to the Spirit's power continually to transform persons' lives. When he began his new position of teaching at Princeton he sought to develop a method of Bible study that would enable him to interpret the New Testament writings "from within the mind of their authors as it were, and then as vitally concerning myself in the core of my personality." Thus the Bible is to Dr. Piper a "means of grace" whereby he hears the "speaking of God" which aids him in understanding himself and the world.

Emile Cailliet is a scholar of international fame. He has published works in ethnology, mysticism, and culture. In 1934 the French Government conferred upon him a medal for "distinguished service in the field of letters." His book, *The Dawn of Personality,* was selected by *The New York Times Book Review* in 1955 as one of the year's "Hundred Best." In his book, *Journey into Light,*[23] Cailliet tells the story of his conversion resulting from his encounter with the Bible. Due to the naturalistic

character of French society in the first part of the twentieth century, he never saw a Bible before he was twenty-
three years old. He characterizes his education as "naturalistic to the core." He left graduate school to volunteer
for the French army in World War I. In the mud and
murder of the trenches he became aware of the utter
inadequacy of his naturalistic philosophy and of a deep
desire for something better. After being wounded and
later discharged from the army he resumed his graduate
work.

The remainder of the story should be told by Dr.
Cailliet himself.

> I had returned to my books, but they were no longer
> the same books. Neither was my motivation the same
> motivation. Reading in literature and philosophy, I
> found myself probing in-depth for meaning. During
> long night watches in the foxholes I had in a strange
> way been longing—I must say it, however queer it
> may sound—for a book that would understand me.
> But I knew of no such book. Now I would in secret
> prepare one for my own private use. And so, as I
> went on reading for my courses I would file passages
> that would speak to my condition, then carefully copy
> them in a leather-bound pocket book I would always
> carry with me. The quotations, which I numbered in
> red ink for easier reference, would lead me as it were
> from fear and anguish, through a variety of interven-
> ing stages, to supreme utterances of release and jubi-
> lation.
>
> The day came when I put the finishing touch to
> "the book that would understand me," speak to my
> condition, and help me through life's happenings. A
> beautiful, sunny day it was. I went out, sat under a

tree, and opened my precious anthology. As I went on reading, however, a growing disappointment came over me. Instead of speaking to my condition, the various passages reminded me of their context, of the circumstances of my labor over their selection. Then I *knew* that the whole undertaking would not work, simply because it was of my own making. It carried no strength of persuasion. In a dejected mood, I put the little book back in my pocket.

At this very moment his wife (who knew nothing of his project) appeared pushing the baby carriage. She, by a very strange set of circumstances, had a Bible with her. Dr. Cailliet continues:

"A Bible, you say? Where is it? Show me. I have never seen one before!" . . . I literally grabbed the book and rushed to my study with it. I opened it and "chanced" upon the Beatitudes! I read, and read, and read—now aloud with an indescribable warmth surging within . . . I could not find words to express my awe and wonder. And suddenly the realization dawned upon me: This *was* the Book that would understand me! I needed it so much, yet, unaware, I had attempted to write my own—in vain. I continued to read deeply into the night, mostly from the gospels. And lo and behold, as I looked through them, the One of whom they spoke, the One who spoke and acted in them, became alive to me. This vivid experience marked the beginning of my understanding of prayer. It also proved to be my initiation to the notion of Presence which later would prove crucial in my theological thinking.

The providential circumstances amid which the Book had found me now made it clear that while it

seemed absurd to speak of a book understanding a
man, this could be said of the Bible because its pages
were animated by the Presence of the Living God
and the Power of His mighty acts. To this God I
prayed that night, and the God who answered was
the same God of whom it was spoken in the Book.[24]

The first part of this chapter pointed out the unique
historical relationship in which the Bible stands to Jesus;
the second part stressed that the biblical revelation is
linked with history in a way that no other revelation
is; the last part has shown that time and time again
persons and groups have had their lives changed in a
remarkable way through the Bible. These lines of evidence lead us to conclude that the Bible is truly unique,
and that it is uniquely connected with the God who really
is!

4

The Uniqueness of the Christian Message

"The gospel is the glory of the Christian faith. No other religion has a gospel."

—Culbert G. Rutenber

In a way all religion aims at the same thing—to bring man to the best possible state or existence. The way that any religion proposes to do this may be called the *message* of that religion. Each message is set against the background of some condition of man that is thought to be unsatisfactory by that religion. A comparison of the Christian message with the messages of other major religions shows its primary content to be utterly unique.

In Zoroastrianism, man's undesirable state results from his choosing the evil way of Angra Mainyu (Shatin or Satan). This choice leads to unfaithfulness, lying, stealing, and wasteful practices. If at the Judgment Day these deeds predominate, then the person will have to dwell forever in the ill-smelling "House of the Lie." He can avoid this tragedy by choosing the right and the good.

An initial choice for the right does not ensure the rightness of all subsequent choices, so ways to overcome the undesirable effects of wrong choices have been provided. Atonement is sought first of all by means of prayers of confession. Sincere penance restores him again to the right relation to his heavenly Father. Such penance involves the resolve not to do the sin again. True confession before the high priest is desirable, but if such is not feasible, the worshipper may make his penitential prayers before the sun, moon, or fire. In addition to confession, other things may be required for ablution, such as corporal punishment, fines, or deeds of righteousness. Zoroaster's role in setting men right is simply that he makes clear through revelation what is right and wrong, the respective results of each, and the urgency of one's making the right choice.

Judaism, too, thinks that what is wrong with man is that he has departed from the will of God. This situation is to be remedied basically by a revelation of God's will and by man's entering into covenant with God. God's will was revealed in the Law which came through Moses. The covenant involves on man's part a recognition of God as supreme and a commitment to do God's will as defined in the Law.

But what if one fails to keep the covenant? According to Jewish teaching, departing from God's Law (sin) may be overcome in various ways.[1] Repentance always is a prerequisite for forgiveness and involves remorse for sin, a turning from sin, a turning back to God and to doing his will, and where possible a restitution to any person wronged. Repentance restores the harmony of the individual with God and ultimately the harmony of all the world.[2] It is a power which God has given to all men. However, repentance is not all that is necessary to overcome sin; atonement is also required. Atonement may be accomplished by suffering, death of the individual, by doing good deeds, and/or the Day of Atonement (Yom Kippur). In the case of suffering and death, there seems to be the idea that pain or loss "pays" for one's sins.

The Day of Atonement originally provided a shedding of blood in sacrifice to "cover" the sin. Since sacrifices are no longer offered, the ritual of the Day itself, which involves confession and prayers, provides the atonement which is needed to make repentance efficacious. The Day of Atonement is still considered the most important day in the Jewish calendar. In the Jewish outlook, the overcoming of sin is the work of *man*. Man must perform the ritual of the Day of Atonement; he atones for his sins through suffering or death, or by his good works; and repentance, without which there is no forgiveness, is also the work of man.

In Islam, the unsatisfactory state of man's existence is traced to man's lack of adequate recognition of and submission to God, the creator of the world. Such a state may be due to ignorance, to unbelief, or refusal to submit. Lack of recognition of God and failure to submit to him will result in perdition. While members of any monotheistic religion which has revealed scriptures have the equipment and ability to submit to God, live the good life, and gain Paradise, the "Straight Path" is that proposed by Islam, according to Muslims. This path is basically accepting the Koran as the revealed Word of God and the teachings of Mohammed as the

most authoritative exposition of his will. Such acceptance involves both moral and ceremonial obligations.

Morally, one is to strive for such qualities as honesty,
social justice, kindness, equality and fair treatment of
all, and help for the poor and needy. The ceremonial
obligations consist of the "Five Pillars" of Islam which,
if faithfully followed, are supposed to bring one into
submission to the will of God. Briefly described, these
pillars[3] are as follow:

(1) *Public Confession*—"There is no god but God, and
Mohammed is the messenger of God." While God is
conceived of as the omnipotent, omniscient Sovereign,
his unity and eternity are also fully emphasized. The
Koran states, "He unto Whom belongeth the sovereignty of the heavens and the earth, He hath chosen
no son nor hath He any partner in the sovereignty"
(25:2). Mohammed is confessed to be God's latest and
therefore his most authoritative messenger. Islam
teaches that the "mere uttering" of the confession
"makes a Muslim of the reciter."

(2) *Prayers*—These are memorized and are to be performed at five set times each day in a strictly prescribed
manner.

(3) *Giving of alms* or "poor-due"—This required religious observance, fundamental to the faith, amounts to
2-3 percent of earnings and is given "as a means of
avoiding the sufferings of the next life," and as an "expiation" or "purification" of what the Muslim retains for
himself of material possessions.

(4) *Fasting*—For the month of Ramadan the devotee
is not to partake of food or drink from dawn to dusk.

(5) *Pilgrimage*—Those who are physically and finan-

cially able are to go to the sacred monument at Mecca at least once in their lifetime.

In Islam it seems that the unsatisfactory element in human existence is simply that the unbelieving and disobedient man is subject to Hell. On the Judgment Day all will be resurrected, and their good deeds will be weighed against their bad ones. If the balance is laden with good deeds, the individual will go to Paradise; if it is laden with bad ones, he must go to Hell.

A Muslim may "make up" for any religious duty which he did not perform at the right time (prayer, fasting, and so on) by doing it at some other time. No expiation is required. If a Muslim violates a prohibition, specific punishments are prescribed which "cover" the sin. Fasting and good deeds of different kinds may also expiate bad deeds. If at the Judgment Day the Muslim's account with God shows a deficit, it will be expiated by a temporary punishment after death. For the one who denies God's existence or unity, Hell is permanent. One is saved (delivered from Hell) by his right beliefs concerning God and his good works. Essentially Mohammed's role was that of a prophet who transmitted the word of revelation concerning God and his will.

The religions which have arisen in India (Hinduism, Jainism, Buddhism, and Sikhism[4]) tend to understand the unsatisfactory state of man's condition in a different way from the religions arising in the Near East. As has been indicated earlier, in India man's problem from which he needs to be delivered is that he is caught in the "wheel of rebirth." Man in this life is subject to change, flux, decay, trouble, and suffering. There is no real remedy for that so long as one lives under the conditions of this world. Neither does death offer any peace or rest because the soul will be reborn into another body. The type of body—human, animal, worm—and the status of the person in the next existence depends on one's *karma*—his thoughts, words, and deeds. In whatever body he may possess he has to undergo a similar round of suffering and contingencies again and again. The problem that each Indian religion seeks to answer from its own slant is, "How can one be delivered from the suffering which individual existence inevitably entails?"

Hinduism, the most well-known Indian religion, is an extremely tolerant one. It recognizes that not all individuals want to be released from individual existence. Therefore, it accepts four "permissible goals in life" [5] that one can choose to follow. If one desires to follow *pleasure,* he may do so without being criticized, so long as he does so according to the generally accepted rules of society. He will, of course, continue to be reborn again and again until in some future existence he comes to realize, on his own, that pleasure-seeking is not a truly satisfying goal.

A second goal that one may choose is to gain *power*—wealth, success, or social position. No blame is attached to the seeker of power, but again it is understood that sooner or later he will recognize, on his own, that there is some higher, more worthy goal for him to seek.

Third, one may make *duty* his goal. In this case he renounces the seeking of personal pleasure or success and aims at the good of others by serving his family, caste, or community. This provides a more satisfying life than seeking pleasure or power, but it still is not the ultimate, as the follower of duty himself will come to realize. The highest and final goal that one can seek is *to be released* altogether from having to be born again. This is *Nirvana*—the best possible state.

Once a person desires to seek release from rebirth, Hinduism recognizes three ways that he may attain it. The first is the *Way of Works*. This basically is the performance of rituals, rites, and duties which add to one's favorable *karma*. How this works out in practice may be seen in the description by Noss:

> Many a Hindu has believed that by sacrificing to the gods and his ancestors, revering the rising sun, keeping the rites and ceremonies that are appropriate at a birth, a death, a marriage, or a harvest, he can acquire enough merit to pass at death into one of the heavens or be reborn as a Brahmin with a real predisposition toward achieving final union with Brahman, the Absolute.[6]

A second way of deliverance in Hinduism is the *Way of Knowledge*. It presupposes that man's implication in the wheel of rebirth is due to his ignorance of the nature of true reality. This idea of ignorance has many variations, but the most well-known form states that it is the illusion of individuality—that individual things have any real existence—that lies at the base of man's trouble. When one comes to see reality clearly he will recognize that individuality is an illusion and everything is really Brahman-Atman—the one, undivided Reality that encompasses everything.

Right beliefs, however, are not sufficient to bring release through the Way of Knowledge. To attain the realm of knowledge where *karma* no longer has any power, one must have "an ecstatic flash of certitude in the midst of deep meditation." [7] The gaining of such knowledge, both intellectual and experiential, requires a long and arduous preparation which may well take an entire lifetime, even after one has gone through the thousands of previous existences that were required to lead him even to desire release.

The third way of deliverance is the *Way of Devotion*. Hinduism is basically polytheistic—the Divine may be conceived of in many different ways, and each conception is valid for the person at that particular stage. In the Way of Devotion one seeks release from rebirth by devotion to a particular god. Devotion is understood as loving adoration which is given in a purely disinterested way.

The concept of works held by those who follow the Way of Devotion may further our understanding. Works, good or bad, have their effect on the soul's future condition (law of *karma*). A good work, done for hope of reward (its "fruit"), may improve the soul's condition by enabling it to stay in some other world for a while, but its good effect spends itself, and the soul is again returned to the cycle of rebirths. But if a good work is done disinterestedly—not for reward but simply out of love for the Adorable—"Then the Adorable Himself enters the heart of the doer and begets therein the virtue of *bhakti* [devotion], and it is this *bhakti* that finally gives eternal salvation." [8]

An interesting feature of the Way of Devotion is its many similarities to Christianity. There is a personal God of love and grace who is the creator of all. Individual souls have a real, independent existence, and their salvation consists of a perpetual, conscious, independent existence at the feet of the Adorable. Moreover, this Supreme God is said to have become incarnate in various forms and for various purposes, as may be seen in the *avatars* of Vishnu. The idea of incarnation will receive further consideration later in this chapter. But here it should be pointed out that, although the Way of Devotion began *prior* to the founding of the New Testament church, there is a real possibility that some of its concepts have been subsequently influenced by Christianity (as well as by Islam).[9]

In Hinduism various means have been proposed to overcome the bad *karma* produced by one's misdeeds. In ancient India different penances were prescribed for various offences. In the most serious cases, the death of the offender was the only thing that could free him from guilt. On some occasions purification from misdeeds was sought through their sacred animal, the cow. Caring for cows, scratching their backs, and even washing oneself with cow urine have been used to absolve guilt. In other cases, fasting, saying of prayers, gifts to Brahmins (priests), sacrifices to the gods, pilgrimages, and fines in the form of public dinners for the caste are the means of expiation and atonement.[10]

Jainism, a religion which arose in India in the sixth century B.C. and has remained confined to that country, seeks to bring release from the chain of rebirths by the way of asceticism. In the Jain understanding of things there is no all-powerful, eternal, Creator God. Neither prayers nor rites are of any help. Salvation is completely self-attained. Souls themselves are immortal, but are burdened by bodies and consigned to endless rebirth until the soul can be purified of all love of or dependence upon the world and all its objects.

This is brought about by a dual course—through rigorous self-discipline whereby the seeker becomes oblivious to all bodily conditions (hunger, discomfort, pain) and through refraining from killing any living thing. Living ascetically, the Jain practices meditation until he gains a "trance-state marked by complete dissociation from the outer world and transcendence of one's own physical states." [11] When so purified the soul is liberated and goes to the top of the universe where it experiences infinite perception, knowledge, power, and bliss.

Buddhism, as we have already seen, teaches that all existence in this world inevitably involves suffering and imperfection. The activating force causing people to be born over and over again is desire or craving. Therefore the state into which man should move is the state of having no desire or craving, no "will-to-live-and-have."

It can be attained by following the eight-fold path that leads to the cessation of suffering. This path leads through moderate ascetic practices to the lessening of the hold of desire on a person and finally to the states of trance and insight where he is "enlightened" and gains liberation from all desires. He no longer feels suffering or experiences earthly pleasure; he does not care whether he lives or dies. He has no concern about his future state, whether he will exist or not, because those desires have been overcome, too.

Such, apparently, was the teaching of Buddha and is followed today by Hinayana Buddhists. In Mahayana Buddhism—the variety which spread into China, Japan, and Korea—new features were incorporated. Gautama Buddha came to be worshiped as a divine being who came to earth from heaven to bring suffering humanity the teaching which would lead to salvation.

Further, many other Buddhas were "discovered" who had, like Gautama, taught the way of enlightenment. There were also other divine beings who came to be worshiped. These were called *Bodhisattvas* or persons who were destined to become Buddhas. They had already freed themselves from desire and were able to enter *Nirvana,* but out of love and compassion they postponed their entrance in order to help others to reach that state.

They were (unlike Gautama in original Buddhism) able and willing to serve as saviors. They existed in "heaven" but were able to hear prayers and come to the aid of men. One of the most popular, Avalokita, is said to have come to earth to aid men over three hundred times in human form and once as a horse. While the *Bodhisattvas* bring aid in this present life, another type of Buddha, the *Dhyani* Buddha, can provide the merit to attain bliss in the future life. One such Buddha is conceived of as able and willing to save and bring one to the Western Paradise, an intermediate stage on the way to *Nirvana,* by faith alone.[12] The works of these Buddhas who share their merits with others may be viewed as a type of atoning activity, that is to say, an activity which helps set people right with Reality. In Hinayana, however, there is no room for atonement at all. One must set himself right by developing certain mental attitudes about life and the world.

In Confucian thought, the unsatisfactory state in which

men found themselves was conceived of primarily in this-worldly terms—the disorder of society with its corruption, exploitation, and violence. Confucius sought through his teachings to restore order in society by producing the correct order in individuals. David H. Smith observes, "Confucianism has little teaching to offer concerning either salvation from troubles and ills of this life, or salvation conceived in terms of a transformed humanity, or salvation as a blissful *post-mortem* existence. Confucianism . . . held forth the ideal of a perfect state [brought about by] the rule of a sage-king, and by acceptance of ethical standards of Confucianism by everyone from king to peasant." [13] Atonement has no place at all in the Confucian system.

This brief survey has shown us that the only beliefs that are even remotely similar to the Christian belief in the incarnation are the beliefs about the descents of Vishnu in the *Way of Devotion* of Hinduism and the *Bodhisattvas* in Mahayana Buddhism. Closer investigation reveals vast differences.

The incarnations of Vishnu are not conceived of as occasions in which the true nature of God is definitively revealed in a truly human life. In fact, several of his incarnations have taken animal form—a fish, a tortoise, a boar, a male lion. In other incarnations he was Gautama Buddha, a dwarf, Rama, and Krishna. What a difference in these stories and the stories of Jesus in the Gospels! In the Gospels Jesus appears as a historical person. The nature and will of God are revealed through a truly human personality. His entire life was a manifestation of the love of God so morally perfect that even his enemies could find nothing of which to convict him. God's revelation in Jesus finds its climax in the self-giving love of the cross for the sins of others. The God of the universe confirms it by actually raising him from the dead.

The *Bodhisattva* idea is quite different from the Christian view of the incarnation in Jesus Christ. First, there are hundreds or even thousands of *Bodhisattvas.* They develop from ordinary beings when the mind "has reached a stage when it can no longer turn back on enlightenment." [14] By this time the soul of the person who becomes a *Bodhisattva* will never again have to be born into a subhuman body, or the body of a woman, or in a low-class family, and the body will always be well-built and free from physical defects.

The *Bodhisattvas* are not sons of God, because, according to Buddhist thought, there is no personal God. The *Bodhisattva* gives help to other beings here on earth "although he knows that the beings are illusory, their troubles are illusory, and his help is illusory." [15] Moreover, the body of the *Bodhisattva* is unreal and fictitious. Conze observes that "little significance is attached to the historical Buddha who is a mere phantom body conjured up by the Dharma-body. Unlike Christianity Buddhism is not a historical religion, and its message is valid independently of the historicity of any event in the life of the 'founder,' who did not found anything, but merely transmitted a Dharma pre-existing him since eternity." [16]

How different is this conception from the message of Christianity which asserts that God, the Creator of the universe, sent his unique Son, not only to reveal in his own personality the true nature of God and man, but also to overcome sin and death by his own life, death, and resurrection in a once-for-all event which has cosmic significance. Real incarnation and once-for-all atonement are unique to Christianity.

Of the world's major religions only Christianity offers definitive revelation through the incarnation of a unique Son of God. No other religion has a central, once-for-all act of atonement where sin is overcome, making it possible for men to be set right. While some religions have individual acts of atonement for specific wrongdoings, in every case the atonement is the *work of man.* This is true even in the Jewish view of atonement.

In startling contrast to the ways by which man is instructed by the various religions to work his way out of his sin and suffering, Christianity proclaims good news. The gospel (good news!) is that *what man could not accomplish through works, God has done for man by sending his Son.* The very assertion that there is an all-good and all-powerful God who ultimately rules the world, who is working out a purpose in it that involves man's highest happiness, and who offers man aid and fellowship is good news that the Buddhist, the Muslim, the follower of Confucius, or the Hindu cannot give.

That God has sent his Son for man's salvation is news that no other religion can give. Man does not have to work his way to salvation by any kind of rites, rituals, rules, prayers, fastings, or disciplines. God has taken the initiative and acted decisively for man's salvation. He has revealed his amazing love authoritatively through a Son. He has reconciled the world unto himself in Christ.

The shed blood (voluntarily given life) of Jesus atoned for sin in a way that the blood of bulls and goats could not do (Heb. 10:4,10). Joachim Jeremias concludes that the only possible reason that Jesus attributed such unlimited atoning power to his death must be that he "died as the servant of God, whose suffering and death is described in Isaiah 53. . . . Because it is life with God and from God that is here given over to death, this death has an unlimited power to atone."[17] Though Christianity has never been able to formulate an official rationale of the atonement, the assertion, "Christ died for our sins," belongs to the essence of the Christian message—a message with no parallel in other religions.

The message of incarnation, atonement, and resurrection is a message based not on myths, but on historical events; not on a painting on a cosmic curtain, but on deeds in history. It is a message that has tremendous power to move men to repentance when it meets with faith and to make new persons out of them, bringing them to fullness of life in fellowship with God and the company of the redeemed. This fellowship is another aspect of the uniqueness of Christianity, but that is another story.

5

The Uniqueness of the Church

"The church is the abiding witness to the manifestation in history of a new reality."

—J. H. Oldham

No religion but Christianity has a church. One might think that this is merely a matter of terminology, that other religions simply have their own names for their particular religious bodies which are the equivalent of the church. Deeper investigation reveals that this is not the case.

While there are some similarities of function between the church and other religious groups, the church possesses a *unique self-understanding*. The world-famous student of comparative religion, the late Joachim Wach, reminds us that the importance of the self-understanding of a religious community must not be overlooked:

The first important concern for the student of religious groups will be to do justice to the self-interpretation of a religious communion. Full meaning is not gained where only the outward and measurable "behavior" is taken into account without regard for the meaning which concepts, attitudes, and acts are meant to convey.[1]

No other religious community thinks of itself in the way the church conceives of itself.

Paul Minear, professor emeritus of biblical theology at Yale, calls our attention to the fact that the church's understanding of itself in the New Testament is presented not so much as a "technical doctrine but as a gallery of pictures"—more than eighty in all.[2] Each picture of the church has something of its own to say, but the uniqueness of the church's self-understanding can be seen clearly by looking at a few of the most important ones.

Perhaps no image of the church is more well-known than Paul's statement that the church is the body of Christ. By this expression much more is meant than a group of disciples who are all followers of Jesus. It emphasizes that members of the church are joined in the closest conceivable relationship with one another and with the living Christ.

If the church is the body of Christ, it is clear that Christianity is never simply an individual matter. It is a "we" religion. Paul declares that believers are "members one of another" (Rom. 12:5). This means, of course, that members care for one another. They "rejoice with those who rejoice and weep with those who weep." Their caring is not merely expressed in sympathy and emotional identification, but is also coupled with concrete acts of consideration and love. The church, as Paul understands it, is a fellowship of love where each gives of himself for the good of the others in the service of God.

The description of the fellowship of the church which Luke gives in Acts 4:32 describes an ideal which expresses itself in some degree wherever the true church is found—"Now the company of those who believed were of one heart and one soul . . . and they had everything in common." Even after the intensity of this first experience passed, the early church continued to exhibit a quality of fellowship that was a marvel to others.[3]

What was the basis or source of this fellowship as Christians understood it? By what means were they brought together in such an intimate way? What opened up the springs of love within, so that they were of "one heart and one soul"? This fellowship derived from the head of the body, Jesus Christ, through whom God made deepest and truest fellowship possible, and through whom he supplied the dynamic of the fellowship.

Jesus is understood as the source of the fellowship, not simply because he was the rallying point around which his followers gathered, but because he broke down the barriers that had prevented truest and deepest fellowship from taking place. Man, who was made for fellowship, does not experience it satisfactorily because of his sin (self-centeredness). His fellowship with God is obstructed or broken because man wants to be autonomous, rather than recognize that his life is a gift from God which is to be given back in loving service and obedience.

His fellowship with other human beings is obstructed or broken because he has neither the time, interest, nor will to care for and communicate with his neighbor. Barriers of race, class, and nation are erected and maintained to protect him from his neighbor. Christians believe, however, that Jesus overcomes sin and redeems man from it. Emil Brunner expresses these ideas as follows:

> . . . the sin from which He redeems us is in fact nothing other than the destruction, the loss, of fellowship with God, which brings in its train destruction of fellowship with men. . . . God's self-communication is the communication of His life, His love, and love is the will to communicate oneself. For this purpose Christ is given to us, that we may live in God's love and draw our life from it. . . . Reconciliation means that this isolation is brought to an end by God's self-communication.[4]

The church in its various views of atonement has provided different ways of understanding *how* Christ overcame sin and restored the communication between God and man, but they are all agreed on one point—Jesus overcame sin through his self-giving love which is seen supremely in his cross-resurrection. As Paul says, "He died for all, that those who live might live no longer for themselves but for him who for their sake died and was raised. God was in Christ reconciling the world to himself" (2 Cor. 5:15,19). God's act of love in Christ lies at the basis of fellowship in the body of Christ.

Gerhard Delling points out that "this unity of the members of the church with one another corresponds to the union between Christ and the 'Father': in this way her absolute uniqueness is established and she is removed from comparison with all other human communities." [5] Man, reconciled to God and experiencing his love, is ready for fellowship on the deepest level.

Christ, the head of the church, has laid the basis for the restoration of fellowship, but he does more. He also provides the spiritual dynamic of the fellowship. The power that made the believers of "one heart and one soul" was in the person of the Holy Spirit who was given to the church by God through the resurrected and exalted Lord (Acts 2:33; 4:31-32).

People had certainly experienced what they understood to be the power of the Divine Spirit *before* the day of Pentecost. The prophet who speaks under "the inspiration of the Spirit" is a common phenomenon, not only in the Old Testament, but in many other religions as well. However, the experience of the followers of Jesus *after* Pentecost was vastly different from "prophetic inspiration." The operation of the Spirit which they began to experience that day was not relegated to certain "inspired" individuals as a temporary manifestation, but was given to the whole body of believers permanently.

The presence of the supernatural Spirit among those who believed in Jesus as Messiah and resurrected Lord was recognized by persons inside and outside the communities.[6] In the churches of Galatia, for example, the experience of the Spirit was so real that Paul could appeal to it for the validation of the genuineness of his message. In the face of the criticism that his gospel was untrue or incomplete, he wrote, "Let me ask you only this: Did you receive the Spirit by works of the law, or by hearing with faith?" (Gal. 3:2). They had received the Spirit and *there was no doubting that!*

The presence of the Spirit in the Christian communities manifested itself in many ways. One of the most constant, universal, and significant was an amazing abundance of love. The Spirit-produced love is the rich and powerful dynamic of the Christian fellowship. In forceful language, born of the experience itself, Paul speaks of the love of God which "has been poured into our hearts through the Holy Spirit which has been given to us" (Rom. 5:5). L. S. Thornton draws out the implications of this language in his book, *The Common Life in the Body of Christ:*

> Now a torrent of water flowing down and moving swiftly across the land . . . is like a living thing. Anything in its pathway is drenched "by" it, immersed "in" it and saturated "with" it. So the Spirit of God is living and active in power; but it is also penetrating to the heart, like water drenching the ground. . . . Our hearts are like gardens, in which streams of divine love, descending from above, penetrate the thirsty ground. . . . The unity of the Body is a living unity created and sustained by the one Spirit.[7]

The gift of the Holy Spirit opened the springs of love in the hearts of the believers in an unprecedented manner. Love is the bond of unity that binds everything together in perfect harmony, and love is produced by the operation of the Spirit. J. Robert Nelson in his study of the church concludes that ". . . apart from the *agapē* love of God, which Paul declares to have been 'poured into our hearts through the Holy Spirit which has been given to us,' the biblical concept of *koinōnia* fellowship is completely unintelligible."[8]

The church does not understand the gift of the Spirit as something that could take place anytime, anywhere, to any people. It was the result of the entrance of God's unique Son into history, his ministry and death, and his resurrection from the dead (John 7:39).[9] By virtue of Jesus' being resurrected from the dead, he became a life-giving Spirit (1 Cor. 15:45) and consequently the head of a new humanity.

The "New Humanity" is one of the images by which the church seeks to express its self-understanding.[10] "New" humanity implies an "old" humanity. The old humanity is the human race before and apart from Christ. Paul contrasts the two humanities in the persons of their respective heads. All men belong to the old humanity by virtue of their earthly, human nature which they inherited from the progenitor of the human race (Adam). But there has appeared a "Second Adam," a second head of a "race" of men. Paul says, " 'The first man Adam became a living being'; the last Adam became a life-giving spirit" (1 Cor. 15:45). Jesus became a life-giving Spirit when he was raised from the dead and entered into a new mode of existence, a mode which Paul characterizes as "spirit." [11]

This mode of existence is one in which those who belong to the body of Christ have already begun to share (because they share in the Spirit) and in which they will share fully one day. The concept of a new mode of existence is related to the early Christian concept of the New Age, the age of the Messiah, the age of the kingdom of God where God's will is done on earth as in heaven. This is an age of eternal life, where death is defeated. It is the age of the resurrection, brought about by the

mighty working of the Spirit of God. This age has already
begun in Jesus. He is the first body of flesh to be liberated from death and transformed into a body of the
Spirit. He is the "first-fruits" of the New Age, and those
joined to him shall experience a resurrection like his
(Rom. 6:5). They in fact already share in the powers
of the age to come (Eph. 1:13-14,19-20; Heb. 6:4-5).[12]

In the light of these ideas we can correctly understand
Paul's statement in 2 Corinthians 5:17 that anyone "in
Christ is a new creation," and James's words about
Christians being a "kind of first fruits of his [God's]
creatures" (Jas. 1:18). Participation in the new humanity
not only transforms the individual's personal life, but
also his relationships with others. In the new humanity
there can be neither Jew nor Greek, slave nor free, male
nor female, for all are one in Christ (Gal. 3:27-28), for
"he has broken down the dividing wall of hostility . . .
that he might create in himself one new man" (Eph.
2:14-15).

It is now apparent how and why the church thinks
of itself as the "people of God, gathered from among
the nations through the redeeming work of the Messiah,
to participate in the new age which he inaugurates." [13]
The New Testament states that in the creation of this
community one of God's principle purposes for his creation of the world finds its fulfillment (Eph. 3:9).

When we consider the church as the body of Christ
and the new humanity brought into being through him
who alone is its resurrected head, then it is clear that
no other religious community understands itself like the
church does. However, there is an image that the Christian church shares with another religion. Jews as well

as Christians think of themselves as the people of God. What does this image mean? How is the church's self-understanding to be distinguished from the synagogue's?

The phrase *people of God,* whether used by Jews or Christians, means that God has chosen them for the accomplishment of his purposes in the world, to be the recipients of his "covenant and promises." God "called" this people to be his own, to organize their lives according to his law and experience communion with him. As their vocation became clearer through the words of the prophets, it was seen that they were called to establish justice and to make the true knowledge of God known to the world. They were to accomplish this task by being a "light to lighten the Gentiles" and a witness to God's deeds and purposes. This could be accomplished only by being a servant who suffers for others (Isa. 42:1-2,6; 43:10).

The sad judgment of the church was that the Jews had rejected the very one in whom God's vocation to Israel was fully embodied and in whom all the promises of God found their fulfillment (2 Cor. 1:20). So long as old Israel failed to recognize Jesus to be the clearest manifestation of God and the fulfillment of the promises made to the fathers, they excluded themselves from the ongoing stream of God's purposes. Their place as witness and instrument is taken over by those who do accept Jesus as the Promised One and confess him as Messiah and Lord (Acts 2:36,39).[14] The consciousness of the church as the people of God to whom now falls the vocation of Israel is clearly expressed in 1 Peter 2:9. After commenting on Israel's rejection of Jesus as Messiah Peter tells the believers, "But you are a chosen race, a royal priesthood, a holy nation, God's own people, that you may declare the wonderful deeds of him who called you out of darkness into his marvelous light."

What was it that distinguished the new people of God (church) from the old (synagogue)? It was precisely the church's experience of reconciliation with God and participation in the promised Spirit, the gift of the new age. This experience had come to them through their faith in and relation to Jesus whom they believed to be the promised Messiah and resurrected Lord.

One other image of the church that appears in the New Testament is important in showing the unique way in which the church understands itself. The church is described as the *temple of the Lord.* The decisive thing about a temple is that it is supposed to be the dwelling place of God (Ps. 132:13-14; Joel 3:17). The New Testament writers are agreed, however, that God "does not dwell in temples made with hands" (Acts 7:48; 17:24). Neither Mount Gerizim nor Jerusalem is of decisive importance anymore (John 4:23). Rather the community of believers is the dwelling place of God (2 Cor. 6:16; Eph. 2:19-22). The reality of God is now experienced within the fellowship of a community of people. Again as in the images of the body and the new humanity, the communal aspect of the church is emphasized. Believers are to be built together as living stones into the temple (1 Pet. 2:5).

A temple is not only the dwelling place of God, but it exists so that God may be worshiped. Every member of the Christian fellowship is a priest who conducts worship of offering spiritual sacrifices (1 Pet. 2:5). These sacrifices are offered both when the community is gathered together and after it disperses.

When the community is gathered together, the spiritual sacrifices are praises to God (Heb. 13:15), teaching, admonition, spiritual songs, and thanksgiving (Col. 3:16). The spiritual sacrifices involve the exercise of certain gifts which the Spirit has bestowed on various members of the community. Paul mentions wisdom, knowledge, faith, healing, working of miracles, prophecy, spiritual discernment, tongues, helpers, administrators (1 Cor. 14)—all of which are to be used for the upbuilding of the body.

The center of this gathered worship was communion with the resurrected Lord who had promised his presence wherever two or three were gathered in his name. This idea of communion with Christ on the part of those gathered in Jesus' name has been called "the clue to the meaning, foundation, content, and aim of the primitive Christian service. . . ." [15] The early Christian prayer *Maranatha,* "O Lord come," is to be understood in this context. It means, "Come and manifest your presence in our midst."

In the new temple, spiritual sacrifices were to be offered often, not only when the community was gathered together. Christians were still priests when they were scattered. Here good deeds and sharing what one had were sacrifices which were pleasing to God (Heb. 13:16). Indeed, one's whole life was to be presented as a living sacrifice as part of one's spiritual worship (Rom. 12:1).

Communion with God is seen as man's highest destiny, the fulfillment of the purpose for which he was made. In Christianity this fulfillment is not attained in isolated individuality, but as a member of a community of persons who also experience communion with each other and grow together as a temple of the Lord, the dwelling place of God in the Spirit (Eph. 2:21-23). Furthermore, the fellowship is not merely hoped-for; it is a present reality as the disciples gather to find the living Christ in their midst.

Whether it be under the figure of the body of Christ, the new humanity, the people of God, or the Temple of the Lord, certain features of the church are emphasized. A new entity in history has been brought into being by God's activity in Christ. The Holy Spirit of the new age is already experienced by a community bound together by love and unity. They enjoy fellowship both human and divine.

No other great religion of the world has a comparable approach to understanding those people who are its adherents. In Hinduism, there is no congregation, no "body" of adherents at all. The paragon of the religious man is the *sannyasin* who has shed all social and worldly ties so that through concentration and meditation on Brahman, he may attain *moksha,* release from individual existence. Worship or devotion is therefore not usually congregational, but is comprised of individual acts [16] (even when done in the company of others at temples, shrines, and pilgrimages) aimed at moving one's self toward release.

Neither is there any idea of an earthly community of the Deity in Zoroastrianism. This religion is highly individualistic, and the only time fellowship or companionship is even alluded to is in some of the descriptions of Paradise. This individuality is reflected in their temple services.

> The Parsi does not consider attendance at the temple indispensable to worship, and places far less store upon it than the faithful Christian does upon church-going. One reason for that fact is that much of the priestly worship at the temple is without special reference to any laity that may be present . . . . But even when assembled in large numbers at the temples, their worship seems to be almost if not quite entirely individual and separate, not collective and united.[17]

When one turns to Buddhism, he does find a religious community that has an important place. The basic confession of faith of the Buddhist is, "I take refuge in the Buddha; I take refuge in the *Dharma* [Teaching]; I take refuge in the *Sangha* [Order]." The *Sangha* is the Buddhist collective body which "authoritatively studies, experiences, and expounds" the teaching of Buddhism.[18] It is a monastic order in which one can be a temporary or permanent member. It maintains an active relationship with the Buddhist laity to whom it transmits and teaches the tradition and is in turn supported by them.

The *Sangha* (which by no means includes all Buddhists) is basically an association for the preservation and perpetuation of Buddha's teaching. The goal of this teaching is to reach *Nirvana*—the cessation of desire. Though *Nirvana* is understood in a variety of ways, in none of them does fellowship with other beings play any role. The *Sangha* does not understand itself as the

"Body of Buddha," or a fellowship of love, or a new humanity, or the community of the future. The Buddhist *Sangha* is in no sense a transcendent reality, but only a functional entity.

In Confucianism there is no distinctive religious community. The followers of Confucian teaching were significantly referred to as the "Confucian School." This school (in addition to education) promoted loyalty to the family and to the state. The family is to be given supreme loyalty. One's whole service is to be devoted to his family.[19] Consequently, worship centered around the family and consisted of simple offerings, prostration, and prayers before household gods and ancestor tablets.

When Confucius worship did come into being several hundred years after his death, it was sponsored by the state. In the seventh century A.D. the emperor ordered the erection of a state temple to Confucius in every prefecture of China and sacrifices offered to him. Later tablets of other distinguished scholars and literary men were also placed in these temples. The services became more elaborate. They were conducted with much ceremonial dignity and solemnity. Music and specially composed prayers were used. The basis of both family and state worship was social and moral, rather than religious. Worship was designed to promote feelings of love, respect, reverence, and duty towards family and state.[20]

The Jews certainly understand themselves as a distinct people chosen by God. There are real differences, however, between the synagogue and the church.

One difference is the difference between promise and fulfillment. The outpouring of the Spirit which the Jews knew only as promise was *experienced* in the church through their acceptance of Jesus as Messiah. This shared experience of the promised Spirit was the basis of a unity unknown to the synagogue. Gerhard Delling observes, "The thought of belonging together in Jewish worship altogether lacks the basis which is decisive for the New Testament, namely that of belonging to Christ and the Spirit, which means that deriving from fulfillment." [21]

Being the recipient of the *fulfillment* of God's promises, promises concerning his purposes for the world, sets the church off from the synagogue. Because the Jewish congregation lacked the experience of fulfillment, "it did not claim to be the direct expression of a transcendent reality." [22] We do not find the Jews, then, speaking of themselves as a new humanity, or of their community as the dwelling place of God in the Spirit.

In Islam one encounters a people organized on a religious basis. In Mohammed's day Arab society was organized on a tribal basis deriving from kinship. He founded a "tribe" based mainly on religion and, as time went on, its religious character became more pronounced. Under the influence of Mohammed, the *ummah* (tribe, people, community) of Arabs became an *ummah* of Muslims—those who submitted themselves to Allah as understood by his prophet. This *ummah* brought together men of "different stocks and nations to form a higher unit." [23]

Muslims are conscious of belonging to a massive worldwide brotherhood where distinctions of race and class are to have no meaning. This is strikingly symbolized in the mosque where all men perform the ritual prayers in unison, shoulder to shoulder, and in the pilgrimages where all wear the same type of white garment. There is also a feeling of solidarity within the religion of Islam. The duties of the individual to the community and *vice-versa* are emphasized. Mercy, kindness, and responsibility for others are taught.

In spite of these similarities to the Christian church there are some real differences. Muslims do not conceive of their *ummah* as being a new humanity, brought into being by the atoning death and transforming resurrection of their founder, which has significance for the whole world. Neither is there any indication that Muslims believe that their *ummah* is the fulfillment of the divine plan of the ages, purposed before the foundation of the world.

The Muslim *ummah* is made up of people who submit themselves to Allah according to the teachings of Mohammed. They hope to gain Paradise after the judgment day, but they do not experience the "powers of the age to come" here and now. The idea of the *ummah*'s being the temple of the Lord in which the Spirit of God dwells, where the presence of God is encountered, and where communion with God takes place is not found in Islam.

Although Mohammed used the figure of the body and its parts to inculcate mutual care and concern within the Muslim community, the *ummah* is not conceived of as the body of Mohammed into which believers are grafted. Theirs is a unity created by individual submission to Allah, not a unity deriving from being "made to drink of one Spirit" (1 Cor. 12:13).

Two things, then, distinguish the Christian community absolutely from every other religious community. First, the church understands itself as a transcendent reality which has been brought into being by the activity of God through his unique Son, Jesus of Nazareth. Secondly, the members believe that they already have begun to experience, through the gift of the Spirit, the communion and fellowship of their Maker and their fellowmen which, in its completely fulfilled form, will constitute their final destiny.

The idea of communion and fellowship is so important because of the basic nature of man. Man is by nature a social animal. Social psychologists call our attention to the fact that "it is only through interaction with other men that he [man] becomes a fully realized human being." [24] One author gives a theological explanation of this empirically observable human fact. The social nature of man is grounded in his creation. "Being God's creature and child, he is by nature more of a socius than of an individual. In seeking satisfactory community with his kind . . . he is merely fulfilling his natural drives and destiny." [25]

Psychologists and sociologists who seek to study man empirically recognize that many of man's most deep-seated problems arise from a sense of alienation. He feels estranged both from his own true self and from his fellowmen. Man's sense of alienation is profusely reflected in modern art and literature. Blanche Gelfant has observed that the modern artist has an almost obsessive concern "over man's aloneness and alienation, over the collapse of his community and the breakdown of tradition, the ineffectuality of love and religion. . . ." [26]

Men do not desire simply to be with other people. Certain social and personal needs such as the social psychologist might describe are, of course, met by persons coming together in groups. But beyond social support and social comparison there is the further desire of human beings for communion with each other. It is to this deeper reality that the psychiatrist Thomas Harris points when he speaks of the "longing for relatedness." [27] One author states that "Gregariousness is too weak a word for the human desire for togetherness. Nothing less than community of the Christian kind will do. That is why man's deepest longing is for God and the Church, the only kind of relations which finally fulfill his personality." [28]

The church has not always lived up to its ideal of fellowship. Nevertheless, it remains a fact that no other great religion has at its heart a self-understanding in which personal relations, the fellowship of love and communion find so central and enduring a place. No other religion provides the means of fellowship which are comparable with those provided by Christianity: (1) atonement and reconciliation with God provided by the complete self-giving love of the founder, and (2) a new experience of the Holy Spirit given by the resurrected and exalted Lord.

The idea of the church as a fellowship of love has not remained just an idea. It has expressed itself in history time and time again. The early fellowship, exhibiting both affection and practical helpfulness, was a source of amazement to the pagan world into which it came. Though certain failures of fellowship cannot be denied, there continue to be significant manifestations of love and fellowship within the church. It is worth asking if any other "organization" has a record that is at all comparable.

The new humanity, of which Christ is the head, has influenced the life of mankind in incomparable ways. It has contributed greatly to a new idea of what it means to be human. The fact that the human ideal now includes humility, self-denial, readiness to forgive and serve, the respect for individual personality, and particular concern for the suffering and oppressed is the result of the church's proclamation of Christ.[29]

Another unique way in which the church has influenced the life of man is pointed out by Alan Richardson. He calls attention to the fact that modern scientific medicine, agriculture, and educational methods arose within the civilization that has been deeply influenced by the church and nowhere else. Further, these benefits were originally carried to other parts of the world by Christian missionaries, and where Christian influence has not been felt today, these benefits are absent.[30]

Let us summarize the main assertions of this chapter. The uniqueness of the church is more than a matter of terminology. No other religious group understands itself in the same way as the church does; no other religious group has the same spiritual life as the church; and no other group has influenced the life of man in the world as the church has. That there are miserable chapters in the history of the church, no one can deny. They are facts of history. They should not blind us, however, to the praiseworthy benefits that the church has brought, or to its unique self-understanding and role in history. These, too, are facts of history.

Conclusion

In Chapter One I took notice of five challenges to the uniqueness of Christianity. What light has been thrown on these by the facts that have been presented in the intervening chapters? How may these challenges be answered?

The challenge which holds that religious beliefs are unimportant runs aground on the fact that our true beliefs affect our actions. For example, if one believes that sickness is caused by evil spirits rather than germs, it will influence what method of treatment he uses for relief. If people believe that the "good of the state" is more important than personal freedom and liberty, it will affect the life of people in society. If one believes that what belongs to his neighbor will be his if he can get it, this surely will have an effect on social relations. If one believes cows to be as sacred as human beings, it will have an effect on the economy. The idea that beliefs are unimportant also implies that truth and facts are either nonexistent, unknowable, or unimportant.

To the challenge of syncretism as represented in the Bahá'í faith it must be answered, first of all, that impartial investigation shows that all great religions can hardly be considered to be "one in essence." The differences in their conceptions of man's basic problem and his highest good are too great and too basic to be explained

110

by "the different needs of the age in which the messengers appear." This might be possible with the religions of Near Eastern origins, but it breaks down when such atheistic religions as Hinayana Buddhism and Jainism are considered.

The second, and most important consideration, is that Christianity is not based on the teachings of a prophet, but on the words and deeds of a unique Son, which were confirmed by events of history. If God really raised Jesus Christ from the dead, then Jesus cannot be simply empaneled in the gallery of the founders of great religions. A Christian cannot become a Bahá'í without violating his understanding of what is true.

In reply to the secular humanist, who holds all religion to be only imaginings painted on the cosmic curtain, we must again point to the facts surrounding one set of pictures. The central pictures of the biblical revelation are not mythical. These pictures are grounded in actual events of history. The remarkable history of the people of God indicates that there *is something behind the curtain!*

When one considers the words and deeds of Jesus of Nazareth and what happened to him, he finds good grounds for believing that there is a supernatural Person who really exists "beyond" the curtain. When one sees what happens in the life of a person who takes the leap of faith, believes that those pictures effectively represent reality, and seeks to build his life upon them, one can scarcely be content in regarding them as purely illusory, any more than the formulae of physics are illusory.

In regard to *relativism* we would first of all assert that reality does have an objective aspect apart from man's apprehension or experience of it. The tree is there, whether I see it or not, or whether or not I call it "tree."

Further, we should award the name "truth" to that description of what actually exists or happens which seems in our best judgment to come nearest to corresponding with what really is. Again, there is a certain intolerance inherent in truth. Failure to adjust ourselves to the world as it really is can have only detrimental consequences. A life built on reality is more enduring and satisfying than one based on error or fantasy. (Eating vegetables *is* better for you than eating cow dung. Penicillin *is* more effective in treating diseases than witchcraft.) If there really is a personal God who establishes the world, loves men, upholds righteousness, and is working out a purpose in the world, then it is "better" to believe in him, learn of his ways, and obey his will than to be ignorant of him or ignore him. On the other hand, if there isn't any such Being, one is simply deceiving himself to live as if there were. Man innately and universally evaluates self-deception in negative terms.

My conviction is that Christianity embodies the truth more than any other world outlook, because its beliefs have been supported by events of history in a way that no other religion has. The history of Israel, the fulfillment of prophecy, and the resurrection of Jesus are instances where reality has supported and confirmed the Christian world view.

Reality's confirmation of the Christian's understanding of it is not restricted to the events of ancient history. The influence of Christianity on subsequent world history is unparalleled.[1] The examples of the power of the Bible mentioned in Chapter 3 show that the message of Christianity still has the power, when it meets with faith, to bring meaning, purpose, and peace to human life. These events, from the first century to the twentieth, confirm the Word which Christianity teaches to be from God. It may be compared, in some respects, to the way that a successful trip to the moon has supported and confirmed the accuracy of the scientist's understanding of the laws of physics.

It should be pointed out that by "Christian world view" we do not mean the total world view and values of Western society, but rather the theology of the Bible. When the Christian message is accepted in a non-Christian culture, all that is of true value in that culture is to be retained and directed toward the worship and service of the one true God. The various expressions of Christianity in different cultures are to be worked out by the church in those cultures, under the leadership of the Holy Spirit, as the Christians enter into dialogue with the biblical revelation. The fullness of God's purpose for the world includes men of every tongue, tribe, and nation who add their particular note (or dance) to the hymn of praise sung by the church universal.

The challenge to Christianity's uniqueness which arises out of direct contact with persons of other religions—many of whom are intelligent, cultured, personable, considerate, and spiritually sensitive—is in some ways the most real challenge of all. Abstractions and generalizations are tested by contact with real human beings. As the East Asia Christian community has clearly seen, "In the last analysis, the Christian encounter is an encounter with men as men, both in their religious life and in their nonreligious life, both in their belief and in their unbelief, both in what they hold to be sacred and in what they hold to be secular." [2]

In such an encounter, blind and arrogant dogmatism on the part of Christians is nothing short of sin. It is both the path of wisdom and true Christian humility for one to participate with the non-Christian neighbor in a common secular life, to accept him with respect as an equal, to cooperate fully in all worthwhile projects, to speak out of one's own experience in the language of everyday life, and to be willing to learn from him and his tradition. We may be sure that God, who has not left himself without a witness in the life of any people, has been at work among those people, too. Whatever truth is present is truth that God has made known.

The Christian himself cannot be proud. The treasure which he bears in a very earthen vessel is not something that he discovered, or figured out, but something that God has done. There is absolutely no room for boasting. But perpetual silence is also sin, for Christ has commanded his followers to be witnesses. And that is precisely what we are to be—not debaters, but witnesses—humble, sensitive, yet faithful and bold witnesses to what we are convinced to be true.

Standing on the foundation of a life of love and service, cooperating fully with all men of goodwill, living in the fullness of the fellowship of the Spirit—we are to point to that series of events in history which find their climax in Jesus Christ, his cross and resurrection. Further, we are to affirm the good news that in Christ the God of all the universe has made himself known and has acted for man's salvation. It has, in fact, happened nowhere else. There is no other Name!

And that's *why I believe in Jesus Christ.*

Notes

Chapter 1

1. (New York: Philosophical Library, 1949), pp. 19-21.
2. Dr. Goodenough, who conducted extensive studies in religion, was not committed to an atheistic position.
3. W. A. Lessa and E. Z. Vogt, *Reader in Comparative Religion: An Anthropological Approach* (New York: Harper & Row, 1965), p. 88.
4. "Religion in Human Life," *American Anthropologist*, LXV (1963), p. 542.
5. See article, "The Rediscovery of Human Nature," in *Time*, Vol. 101, No. 14 (April 2, 1973), pp. 78-81.
6. According to the U. S. Headquarters (Wilmette, Ill.) the number of local Bahá'í Assemblies in the United States increased from 440 in 1969 to 877 in 1973. The number of localities where Bahá'ís reside in the United States increased from 2,533 to 6,200. Worldwide there are Bahá'ís in 333 countries and territories.
7. *The Hindu View of Life* (New York: The Macmillan Company, n.d.), p. 37.
8. *The Validity of the Christian Mission* (New York: Harper & Row, 1972), pp. 23-44.
9. *Ibid.*, p. 44.

Chapter 2

1. Brief descriptions of the primary sources of the life and teaching of each founder are given in Appendix I.

2. The sketch which follows depends primarily on A. V. Williams Jackson, *Zoroaster the Prophet of Ancient Iran* (New York: AMS Press Inc., 1965).

3. *New Catholic Encyclopedia,* s.v. "Zoroaster."

4. J. Duchesne-Guillemin, *The Hymns of Zarathustra* (Boston: Beacon Press, 1952), p. 5.

5. S. V. McCasland, G. E. Cairns, and D. C. Yu, *Religions of the World* (New York: Random House, 1969), p. 129.

6. The *Gathas* are generally held to be the work of Zoroaster himself. They may be read in J. Duchesne-Guillemin's translation entitled *The Hymns of Zarathustra, op. cit.*

7. This sketch of Buddha is drawn from E. J. Thomas, *The Life of Buddha as Legend and History* (London: Routledge & Kegan Paul LTD, 1949), and Herman Oldenberg, *Buddha: His Life, His Doctrine, His Order,* trans. W. Hoey (London: Williams and Norgate, 1882).

8. Oldenberg, *op. cit.,* p. 106.

9. *Ibid.,* p. 107.

10. Quoted by Oldenberg, *ibid.,* p. 107.

11. A. Foucher, *The Life of Buddha According to the Ancient Texts and Monuments of India,* trans. S. B. Boas (Middletown: Wesleyan University Press, 1963), p. 243, and J. Kashyap, author of Chapter 1 in K. Morgan's *The Path of the Buddha* (New York: Ronald Press, 1956), pp. 3, 10-23.

12. It is held that there were many Buddhas before Siddhattha and that many will come afterward.

13. Kashyap, *op. cit.,* p. 19.

14. *Ibid.*

15. *Ibid.*

16. For Confucius we follow H. G. Creel, *Confucius and the Chinese Way* (New York: Harper & Row), 1960.

17. *Ibid.* p. 55.

18. *Ibid.,* p. 124.

19. See Appendix I for the problem of sources for Jesus.

The scholars whose works we follow avoid both extreme skepticism and extreme literalism in their interpretations. They are A. M. Hunter, *The Work and Words of Jesus* (Philadelphia: The Westminster Press, 1950); Vincent Taylor, *The Life and Ministry of Jesus* (New York: Abingdon Press, 1955); and C. H. Dodd, *The Founder of Christianity* (New York: The Macmillan Company, 1970).

20. Taylor, *op. cit.,* p. 81.

21. Dodd, *op. cit.,* p. 163. Dodd is referring to the fact that at Jesus' crucifixion all his followers deserted Jesus and fled. It was only their coming to believe that Jesus was alive again that brought them back together (pp. 96f.).

22. *Ibid.,* pp. 37-52.

23. Taylor, *op. cit.,* pp. 148-151, 197-199, and J. Jeremias, *New Testament Theology,* trans. John Bowden (New York: Charles Scribner's Sons, 1971), p. 299.

24. Jeremias, *op. cit.,* pp. 63-68. Such usage certainly implies a sense of uniqueness, whether or not it implies a belief in his own preexistence.

25. Hunter, *op. cit.,* p. 84.

26. Taylor, *op. cit.,* p. 60.

27. Our guides for the life of Mohammed are Tor Andrae, *Mohammed: The Man and His Faith,* trans. T. Menzel (New York: Harper & Row, 1960) and W. M. Watt, *Muhammad: Prophet and Statesman* (London: Oxford University Press, 1961).

28. Quoted by Andrae, *op. cit.,* pp. 154f.

29. Watt, *op. cit.,* p. 229.

30. Andrae, *op. cit.,* pp. 173-175.

Chapter 3

1. It is undeniable that these documents all claim to be the immediate expression of the apostles' testimony as eyewitnesses. O. Cullmann, *The Early Church* (Philadelphia:

Westminster Press, 1956), pp. 75-81, 89.

2. *Ibid.,* pp. 76, 81.

3. *Interpreter's Dictionary of the Bible,* s.v. "Jesus Christ."

4. Gurdon C. Oxtoby, *Prediction and Fulfillment in the Bible* (Philadelphia: Westminster, 1966), pp. 66-68. Note that "fulfill" as it is used in the New Testament has a variety of meanings. It may mean prediction, but it may also involve a correspondence of phraseology or ideas. The Scripture cited from the Old Testament may be illustrative, or simply add to perspective.

5. Gerhard von Rad, *Old Testament Theology,* trans. D. M. G. Stalker (New York: Harper & Row, 1965), II, pp. 369-374.

6. See Chapter 1.

7. G. E. Wright, *God Who Acts* (London: SCM Press, 1956), p. 57.

8. Rolf Rendtorf, "The Concept of Revelation in Ancient Israel," in *Revelation as History,* ed. W. Pannenberg (New York: The Macmillan Company, 1968), pp. 45-47.

9. *Ibid.,* p. 47. Though the idea of "revelation through history" has recently been criticized, I believe that it can be maintained.

10. See for example John Bright's *History of Israel* (Philadelphia: Westminster Press, 1972).

11. *Revelation and Reason,* trans. Olive Wyon (Philadelphia: Westminster, 1946), p. 84.

12. Wright, *op. cit.,* p. 40, Brunner, *op. cit.,* p. 84; Alan Richardson, *Christian Apologetics* (London: SCM Press, 1955), p. 196. Compare with von Rad's statement, "The way in which the prophet gives the exact time in which they received certain revelations, dating them by events in the historical and political world, and thereby emphasizing their character as real historical events has no parallel in any other religion." *Old Testament Theology, op. cit.,* p. 363.

13. H. Van Der Loos, *The Miracles of Jesus* (Leiden: E. J. Brill,

1968), p. 699. See also Ulrich Wilkens, "The Understanding of Revelation Within the History of Primitive Christianity" in *Revelation as History,* ed. W. Pannenberg (New York: Macmillan, 1968), pp. 76f.

14. P. Althaus quoted in W. Pannenberg, *Jesus—God and Man,* trans. L. Wilkins and D. Priebe (Philadelphia: Westminster, 1963), p. 100.

15. Bernard Ramm, *Special Revelation and the Word of God* (Grand Rapids: Eerdmans, 1961), pp. 112f.

16. *Pastors All* (Nashville: Gideons International, n.d.), pp. 9-10.

17. *Ibid.,* pp. 6-7.

18. *The American Bible Society Record,* Vol. 116, No. 8, p. 148.

19. S. L. Greenslade, *The Cambridge History of the Bible, The West from the Reformation to the Present Day* (Cambridge: at the University Press, 1963), pp. 394, 401.

20. Clarence W. Hall, "The Book of Shimabuku" (New York: American Bible Society, 1948).

21. James Ray, "The Secret of Our Survival," *Guideposts,* July, 1973, pp. 1-6.

22. Vol. LXIII, No. 9 (Feb. 27, 1946), pp. 266-268; No. 10 (March 6, 1946), pp. 299-301; No. 11 (March 13, 1946), pp. 334-336; No. 12 (March 20, 1946), pp. 362-364.

23. (Grand Rapids: Zondervan Publishing House, 1968).

24. *Ibid.,* pp. 16-18.

Chapter 4

1. See W. O. E. Oesterley and G. H. Box, *The Religion and Worship of the Synagogue* (London: Sir Isaac Pitman and Sons, 1911), pp. 270-274. Also *Encyclopedia Judaica,* s.v. "Atonement."

2. *Encyclopedia Judaica,* s.v. "Repentance."

3. A longer description of these may be found in Caesar

Farah's _Islam: Beliefs and Observances_ (Woodbury: Barron's Educational Series, Inc., 1968), pp. 134-150.

4. Sikhism is basically a combination of Hindu and Muslim conceptions and does not contain any significant ideas which are not found in these two religions.

5. John B. Noss, _Man's Religions,_ fourth edition (London: Collier-Macmillan Limited, 1969), pp. 191-192.

6. _Ibid.,_ p. 192.

7. _Ibid.,_ p. 196.

8. _Hastings' Encyclopedia of Religion and Ethics,_ s.v. "Bhakti-marga."

9. _Ibid._

10. _Hastings' Encyclopedia, op. cit.,_ s.v. "Expiation and Atonement (Hindu)."

11. Noss, _op. cit.,_ p. 117.

12. _Ibid.,_ p. 165.

13. _Dictionary of Comparative Religion,_ ed. S. G. F. Brandon (New York: Charles Scribner's Sons, 1970), p. 552.

14. _Ibid.,_ p. 145.

15. E. Conze in D. T. Suzuki, _On Indian Mahayana Buddhism_ (New York: Harper & Row, Publishers, 1968), p. 23.

16. _Buddhist Thought in India_ (Ann Arbor: The University of Michigan Press, 1967), p. 232.

17. _New Testament Theology,_ trans. John Bowden (New York: Charles Scribner's Sons, 1971), p. 299.

Chapter 5

1. _The Comparative Study of Religions_ (New York: Columbia University Press, 1958), p. 124.

2. _Interpreter's Dictionary of the Bible,_ s.v. "The Idea of the Church."

3. A. Harnack, _The Mission and Expansion of Christianity,_ trans. J. Moffatt (New York: Harper & Brothers, 1961), pp. 147-198.

4. *The Christian Doctrine of the Church, Faith and the Consummation,* trans. D. Cairns and T. H. L. Parker (Philadelphia: The Westminster Press, 1962), p. 21.

5. *Worship in the New Testament,* trans. Percy Scott (Philadelphia: The Westminster Press, 1962), p. 180.

6. Harnack, *op. cit.,* pp. 199-218.

7. (London: Dacre Press, fourth edition, 1963), p. 94.

8. *The Realm of Redemption* (Chicago: Wilcox & Follett Co., 1951), p. 58.

9. Thornton, *op. cit.,* p. 429.

10. Minear, *op. cit.,* p. 615. Harnack, *op. cit.,* pp. 240-265 shows that this conception continued to be important to the church's self-understanding in the second and third centuries.

11. Neil Q. Hamilton, *The Holy Spirit and Eschatology in Paul* (Edinburgh: Oliver and Boyd Ltd., 1957), pp. 14ff.

12. Hamilton, *op. cit.,* pp. 19-21.

13. Minear, *op. cit.,* p. 608.

14. Nelson, *op. cit.,* pp. 8-10.

15. Delling, *op. cit.,* p. 15.

16. Brandon, *op. cit.,* p. 653.

17. *Hastings' Encyclopedia, op. cit.,* s.v. "Worship (Parsi)."

18. Richard Gard, *Buddhism* (New York: George Braziller, 1961), p. 167.

19. Noss, *op. cit.,* p. 286.

20. *Hastings' Encyclopedia, op. cit.,* s.v. "Worship (Chinese)."

21. Delling, *op. cit.,* p. 178.

22. *Ibid.,* p. 175.

23. *Shorter Encyclopedia of Islam,* ed., H. A. R. Gibb and J. H. Kramers (New York: Cornell University Press, 1965), p. 604.

24. G. Watson and D. Johnson, *Social Psychology: Issues and Insights,* second edition (Philadelphia: J. B. Lippincott Company, 1972), p. 79.

25. Nels Ferré, *The Christian Understanding of God* (New York: Harper & Brothers, 1951), p. 39.

26. Blanche H. Gelfant, *The American City Novel* (Norman:

University of Oklahoma Press, 1954), p. 21.

27. *I'm OK—You're OK* (New York: Harper & Row, 1967), p. 218.

28. Ferré, *op. cit.*, p. 39.

29. H. Berkhof, *Christ the Meaning of History,* trans. Lambertus Buurman (Richmond: John Knox Press, 1966), pp. 88-89.

30. In a letter explaining the idea expressed in his *Christian Apologetics,* pp. 115-116.

Conclusion

1. O. A. Piper, *God in History* (New York: The Macmillan Co., 1939).

2. "The Christian Encounter with Men of Other Faiths," Statement Adopted by a Commission of the E.A.C.C. Assembly, Bangkok, 1964, quoted in *Christ and Humanity,* ed. Iver Asheim (Philadelphia: Fortress Press, 1970), p. 182.

Appendix

A Description of the Primary Sources of Information About the Lives and Teachings of the Founders of Great Religions Studied in Chapter 2

ZOROASTER

The sacred scriptures of the Zoroastrians is the *Avesta*.[1] The *Avesta* is comprised of the remains of a much larger body of writings which was destroyed during the invasion by Alexander the Great (330 B.C.). When Persia began to recover her independence (third century A.D.) a search was made for all surviving sacred writings, and the sacred traditions existing only in oral form were written down. In the next century the collection, consisting of a fixed number of books, was declared canonical. These writings were largely destroyed by the Muslims who ordered them all to be burned when they overran Persia. The present-day editions of the *Avesta* are the portions that the faithful Zoroastrians were able to save. The oldest known manuscripts that exist today date back to the 12th—14th centuries A.D.

These scriptures of the Zoroastrians are comprised mainly of four parts. (1) The *Yasna* is made up of seventy-two hymns which are chanted in connection with the preparation of *Haoma*, a sacred drink used in a worship ceremony. (2) The *Vispered* is a supplement to the *Yasna* and contains other prayers or worship formulae. (3) The *Yasts* is comprised of twenty-

one hymns addressed to angels and heroes of ancient Iran.
(4) The *Vendidad* or "law against deamons" contains priestly
regulations having to do with purifications, and expiations.
A few other minor portions of writings complete the *Avesta.*

The most authentic information about Zoroaster comes
from seventeen hymns embedded in the *Yasna.* These hymns,
called *Gathas,* are written in a different style from the rest
and are generally held to be the work of the founder himself.[2]
The information they give is very scanty. Other parts of the
Avesta provide traditions about Zoroaster. This information
is supplemented by the *Denkart.* The *Denkart* is not part of
Zoroastrian scripture, but an encyclopedia of the religion written in the ninth century A.D. when there was a brief revival
of Zoroastrianism in Persia. Book vii relates the life of Zoroaster, according to legend.

BUDDHA

There are two great branches of Buddhism—Hinayana and
Mahayana. Hinayana (or the Theravada) is recognized as the
branch that seeks to stay closest to the teachings of the historical Buddha, and therefore it is from the scriptures of this
group that we seek to get our information about Buddha.

The Hinayana scriptures are divided into three groups: the
Suttas, or discourses (also contains some legends), the *Vinaya,*
or disciplinary rules for the monks, and the *Abhidhamma,* or
a philosophical systematization of the doctrines of the *Suttas.*
They are written in the Pali language. All three parts are
supposed to contain utterances of Buddha, but there is much
other material in them as well, such as discourses by disciples
of Buddha or of the revisers of the Buddhist tradition. E. J.
Thomas points out that, "In the Dhamma [Suttas] and Vinaya,
we possess, not a historical framework containing discourses,
as in the case of the Gospels, but simply discourses and other

dogmatic utterances, to which traditions and commentarial legends have later become attached." [3]

The traditions of Buddha's teachings were preserved in oral form until the third Buddhist Council held over two hundred years after his death. The result of this long process of oral transmission is stated by Thomas, "In the present state of our knowledge we cannot in any instance declare that Buddha said so and so. The fact that we start from is that we have a collection of documents, which were held some two centuries after Buddha to contain his utterances." [4] The events of Buddha's life are even less well attested than his teachings. Our knowledge of these events is based on accounts apparently written down later than the teachings of Buddha.[5]

CONFUCIUS

The scriptures of Confucianism consist of the "Five Classics" and the "Four Books." Of the Five Classics, three were probably written before Confucius's time; two—*Annals of Spring and Autumn* and the *Book of Rites*—after his time. *The Annals of Spring and Autumn,* sometimes considered to have been compiled by Confucius, is comprised of two parts. The first probably antedates Confucius and the other, a commentary, which preserves some information about the sage, probably comes from about 300 B.C. The *Book of Rites* may contain some earlier material, but in its present form dates from the second century B.C.[6]

The Four Books consist of *The Analects, The Great Learning, The Doctrine of the Mean,* and *The Book of Mencius. The Analects* contain sayings of Confucius and his disciples which were written down probably in the generation after Confucius's death.[7] It is held to be the most reliable source of information about Confucius.

The Great Learning and the *Doctrine of the Mean* come from the third and second centuries B.C. respectively, and do not provide much authentic information on Confucius. The *Book of Mencius,* however, is a valuable source. Mencius was a Confucian philosopher who lived about a century after Confucius. The book which bears his name preserves tradition about Confucius "in some detail and in a very early form." [8]

JESUS

The main sources of information about Jesus are the Gospels of the New Testament. Jesus is referred to in some extracanonical documents of the first and second centuries such as the works of Josephus and Tacitus.[9]

Modern critical scholars date the Gospels as follows: Mark, 65-70 A.D.; Matthew, c. 85; Luke, 85-90; and John, 90-100 A.D. From the death of Jesus until the first writing down of the information about him (about 35 years) the material about Jesus was preserved in the preaching and teaching of his disciples.

In evaluating the sources, scholars vary from extreme skepticism (we can know practically nothing about Jesus) to extreme literalism (we can successfully harmonize all the Gospel accounts into one, unified, purely historical narrative). The account of Jesus presented in Chapter 2 followed scholars who avoid both extreme skepticism and extreme literalism.

MOHAMMED

There are basically two kinds of primary sources of information about Mohammed—the Koran and some literature from the third and fourth centuries of the Muslim era. The Koran is composed of the words of Mohammed which he is said to have received from God. The other literature is made up of a life of Mohammed by Ibn Hishām, the *Annals* of at-Tabari, the *Tabaqāt* of Ibn Sa'd, the *hadith* (sayings of Mohammed transmitted orally until over one hundred years after his death), and the *maghāzī* literature of the campaigns.

There are some problems involved in the use of these sources. According to one recent scholar, "Mohammed is not the well-known figure he is often thought to be. On the contrary, at many crucial points our sources are entirely silent, and at many others their reliability and the method of their use are so much in doubt that little can be said with certainty." [10] However, a critical, historical methodology can provide us with a trustworthy account of his life.

Appendix

Notes

1. *Hastings' Encyclopedia of Religion and Ethics,* s.v. "Avesta."
2. *Encyclopedia Britannica,* s.v. "Zoroaster."
3. E. J. Thomas, *The Life of Buddha as Legend and History* (London: Routledge & Kegan Paul LTD, 1949), pp. xix, 249f.
4. *Ibid.,* p. 251.
5. For example, see the Sanskrit works entitled the *Mahāvastu* and the *Lolita-vistara,* as well as the Pali introduction (5th cen. A.D.) of the *Jataka* tales. *Ibid.,* pp. xx f., 274.
6. J. B. Noss, *op. cit.,* p. 280.
7. H. G. Creel, *op. cit.,* p. 271.
8. *Ibid.,* p. 10.
9. C. Milo Connick provides a convenient summary of this information in his book *Jesus: The Man, the Mission, and the Message* (Englewood Cliffs: Prentice Hall, 1963), pp. 58-61.
10. Charles J. Adams, *A Reader's Guide to the Great Religions* (New York: The Free Press, 1965), p. 299.